Saving the Channel Ports 1918

'YOU ARE THE ONLY FORMED BODY OF TROOPS, (1st AUSTRALIAN DIVISION) BETWEEN HERE AND THE CHANNEL PORTS.'

Lieut-General Sir Charles Harrington, Chief of Staff, 2nd Army, addressing Australian officers on Hazebrouch Railway Station, Belgium, 14th April 1918.

The Author, off duty in the Reserve Line at Ypres before the German grand offensive March 1918.

Saving

the

Channel Ports

1918

W. D. JOYNT, 𝔙.𝕮.

WREN PUBLISHING

Published 1975

Hardback Edition ISBN   0 85885 202 0
Paperback Edition ISBN   0 85885 203 9

© W. D. Joynt, 1975

Printed at The Dominion Press, Joseph Street, North Blackburn,
Australia 3130

At the Peace Conference in Paris in July 1918, when Woodrow Wilson and the Council of Ten (including Britain) were denying Australia a say in determining the peace terms, a Parisian newspaper *(Le Matin)* came out strongly in advocating that the voice of Mr W. M. Hughes, Prime Minister of Australia, should be given a hearing, and printed a long article of an interview with Mr Hughes in the course of which the paper wrote:

'. . . The men and women of France, and I may add, the men of the British Army, too, will allow free speech to the spokesman of those who *saved the day*, and saved the campaign on that awful day to the east of Amiens, not yet a year old.'

Le Matin

Contents

List of Illustrations and Maps

Preface

During the great German offensive on the Western Front in March, April and May 1918, which resulted in the partial collapse of the British Second and Fifth Armies, there was an official conspiracy of silence regarding the work of the Australian troops who largely retrieved the situation at this time.

General Sir John Monash wrote to his wife:

> Our press correspondents are forbidden even to mention the fact that Australians are in this vicinity [in front of Amiens], and several long cables which I know are ready to go to Australia have been held up in consequence. The full story, therefore, of what Australians and New Zealanders have done to entirely retrieve the situation will probably not be known to the world at large until the news has become stale.*

As sufficient time has surely passed, by now, let honour be to whom honour is due. That is my main object in publishing this book. It is not written with the intention of denigrating the British Army—far from it. It is written entirely for the purpose of making known the great achievements of the A.I.F. in saving Amiens and the Channel Ports when part of the British Second Army, as well as the Fifth Army, gave way. Resistance to the enemy's advance on those fronts

---

* F. M. Cutlack ed., *War Letters of General Monash* (Sydney, 1934), p. 231.

had broken down except in isolated cases where individual British units still fought it out with the tenacity of tradition.

On 7 November 1920, at a rededication and commemorative service in Amiens Cathedral at which representatives of all the Allied nations were present, the Bishop of Amiens and Marshal Foch, Generalissimo of the Allied Armies, both paid tribute to Australia troops.

The Bishop of Amiens:

> We bow to you Messieurs les Australiens, for the magnificent deeds that you did in those days, now happily at an end, for your country and for France, and for the victory of hope and sanity . . . The soil of France is transfigured to a new divinity by your sacrifices. In the whole of history we cannot find an army more marvellous in its bravery, and in the war there was none that contributed more nobly to the final triumph.

Marshal Foch:

> We intend today in Amiens, to express to you and the Commonwealth of Australia our gratitude . . . Although our task was never easy, it was made less difficult by the patriotism and the passionate valour of the Australians which served as an example to the whole world! That wonderful attack of yours at Villers-Bretonneux was the final proof, if any were needed, that the real task of the high command was to show itself equal to its soldiers. You saved Amiens! You saved France! Our gratitude will remain ever and always to Australia.

Acknowledgements

In writing this book I have drawn on a number of sources for factual and documentary material.

My greatest debt is to C. E. W. Bean's *Official History of Australia in the War of 1914–18,* vols V and VI: *The A.I.F. in France 1918.* Only the lengthy quotations from this source are given page references, but the interested reader may readily locate other passages by means of the history's excellently detailed indexes. Permission for such use, and for the reproduction of a number of maps, was kindly granted by the Australian War Memorial, Canberra. I am grateful also for War Memorial permission to peruse diaries and records, and to reproduce some photographs from its collection.

Lieutenant-General Sir John Monash's *The Australian Victories in France in 1918* and war letters provided useful material.

If I should have inadvertently borrowed from any works not given due credit here or elsewhere, I offer my sincere apologies.

For their inspiration and support in this project my thanks go to Air Chief Marshal Sir Frederick Scherger, K.B.E., C.B., D.S.O., A.F.C.; Emeritus Professor Sir Arthur Amies, C.M.G., Patron, Rats of Tobruk Association, Victorian Branch; Brigadier Sir William Hall, C.B.E., D.S.O., E.D., National President, Returned Services League of Australia; Major-General S. M. McDonald, C.B.E., M.C., E.D., former Commander

3rd Division, Citizen Military Forces of Australia; Colin Keon-Cohen, Esq., o.b.e., State President, Returned Services League of Australia, Victorian Branch; Lieut-Colonel T. E. Williams, o.b.e., e.d., President, United Service Institute of Australia; Major H. H. Yoffa, Hon. Librarian, United Service Institution, Victoria; W. Freeman, Esq., Manager, Presbyterian Book Room, Melbourne, for his advice and helpful introductions to English and Australian Publishers who gave me much support in bringing out this book.

Introduction: the situation in 1918

Following the Russian Revolution in October 1917 and the subsequent peace agreement between Germany and Russia on 3 March 1918, all the German prisoners of war held by Russia—about 1,800,000—together with most of the German Eastern Front Army, became available for transfer to Germany's Western Front. This made the position of the Germans, as far as numbers were concerned, better than at any previous time in the war, giving them 192 divisions on the Western Front against 175 divisions of the Allies.

On 21 March 1918, the Germans launched their Spring Offensive with forty-four divisions, supported by another forty at the junction of the British and French Armies, on a front of forty miles from Arras to the Oise, which was held by the British Third and Fifth Armies. Although the British had been expecting the attack and for nearly three months had been erecting defences, they were still unprepared in some places for such a gigantic offensive. Furthermore, British Army morale in some units was not particularly high.

I returned from two weeks leave in England at the end of January and, travelling on the leave boat-train from London to Dover to embark for Boulogne, I spoke to two English officers. They told me that they dreaded going back to France to face the huge German offensive expected. One even said, 'We are going to get a terrible beating.' This sort of talk

1

amazed me—it was so different from the Diggers' thoughts. Australian officers were hurrying back to France to 'be in it' and the Diggers were actually looking forward to it all. For the whole of the war they had been used as attacking troops and now it was to be their turn to sit behind prepared defences and shoot down the oncoming enemy. I heard a Digger say, 'This will do us for a change.' The Australian morale was never so high.

Our officer promotion system was very different from the English. The majority of Australian junior, and many senior, officers had served in the ranks and had won their promotion to commissioned rank by sheer merit, being mostly the pick of the N.C.O.s: experienced and war-tried sergeants, proven leaders of men chosen by character to be sent to officers' training schools. This gave satisfaction to the troops they commanded and also guaranteed an efficient officer corps.

On the contrary, the English method of appointing junior officers was mostly a matter of influence and an English public school background. A Manchester merchant who entertained me whilst I was on leave told me that his son had just been called up and 'I hope to get him a Commission because I know someone who knows someone at the War Office'! Promotion from the ranks was very rare and, if it did occur, the one promoted was always sent to another unit, never to his own. One reason for this method of creating officers was the English caste system that still existed. So strong was this consciousness of lower, middle and upper classes that the English 'Tommy' had no confidence in the men of his own class and preferred to serve under officers from the so-called upper class. The result was the appointment of a lot of junior officers unfit for command because of their inexperience and their inability to lead men in a crisis.

Within a week of the opening of the German offensive

the Fifth Army was in a state of disintegration but the Third Army, although badly shaken, still remained intact. It had retired, fighting rearguard actions, to conform with the retreating Fifth Army on its right. Some bad gaps existed in its front but it was still 'under command' — whereas the Fifth Army had only one corps still fighting. The two Regular cavalry divisions with the Fifth Army did a magnificent job, keeping their formation throughout and acting up to the best traditions of the British Regular Army.

Dr C. E. W. Bean says that officers of the French Army near the British Fifth Army kept sending disturbing news of the Fifth Army's 'exhaustion and disorganization'. They complained that 'not merely did it fail to exhibit the "bulldog tenacity" expected from British infantry in defence but its organization and system of communication were so shattered that it was "incapable of serious resistance"'. This undoubtedly was due in the main to the poor quality of some of its officers, particularly the junior ones. Some of the senior divisional officers were also most incompetent. Australian troops found an English general alone, hiding in the woods and crying. The poor showing amongst the junior officers was partly due to the system of officer appointments already described, and also the lack of fraternal feeling between officers and men. The accepted rule in the British Army was that even in the front line, officers' Messes should be maintained with at least some faint reflection of the aloofness to which the officer-class in England was accustomed. Even in the trenches,where possible, officers of each company messed together whereas Australian tradition was for officers in the front line to take the same food and drink as their men, and certainly not to leave the trenches to have their meals as a Mess.

At the second army officers' training school I attended as a second lieutenant after the First Battle of the Somme in 1916, the School Commandant announced one evening after

Mess: 'Tomorrow night the subject of the lecture will be Discipline.' He added, 'So important is this subject that I have invited Major-General ———— to come from Army Headquarters to give this lecture. He was a company commander at Mons and I feel he is the most qualified man I know to speak to us on this vital subject of discipline.' As a result we were all keyed up with expectation and listened intently to what the General had to say. At the school there were five platoons of English officers and three Australian platoons, each of forty men. I don't know what the English officers thought of the lecture but we Australians were not at all impressed. In the course of the talk the General said: 'As an example of what I mean—if I had a brother and he was in the ranks, rather than be seen walking down the street talking together I would sooner lose £5!' (A lot of money in those days!)

To many, the breakdown of the British Fifth Army was a complete mystery. General Pétain, commanding the French Army, was puzzled as to why the Fifth Army had not made a firm stand, and gossip emanating from British G.H.Q contrasted the fluidity of the Fifth Army with the stubbornness of the Third and wondered at the reason. French Army criticisms casting the blame on General Gough for the poor showing of his army are not altogether borne out by the histories of some of the German units, which refer to the stubbornness of the Third and Fifth Armies' defence. Undoubtedly there were many cases in which individual British regiments did well but the fact remains that as a whole, the Fifth Army failed to measure up to British tradition. Was this partly due to the British Army set-up, which did not encourage junior officers to express their own individuality and at times act independently but made them always 'wait for orders'?

In the winter of 1917 after the dreadful fighting on the Somme following Pozières, I was detached with my platoon to do a salvage job recovering piles of artillery shells left behind by our advancing artillery units. It was a 'behind the lines' job and I was attached for rations to a battalion in the 61st Division. I became friendly with the English Colonel, who occasionally used to visit me and watch my platoon at work. He said to me one day that he was amazed at the manner in which I, only a lieutenant, carried on without orders. 'I wish our junior officers were permitted to act without always having to refer to higher authority [the platoon commander having to ask his company commander, the company commander having to ask his battalion commander, etc. before taking action], and were encouraged to use their own initiative without waiting for orders. If our army worked more like you Australians and our men showed the same initiative the war would be over in six months.' To me this was a startling statement from a British colonel!

But it was not only the English junior officers who lacked drive: their superior officers were often at fault. In some cases it was due to the aristocratic outlook of the generals, many of them considering that it was 'bad form' to be too concerned personally in the training of their troops: 'That's a job for others to do!' They encouraged the belief amongst their junior officers that they should concentrate on being gentlemen; they did not train them to use their initiative so that they could lead their men in a crisis.

The French Army never did hold a high opinion of English officer efficiency. Napoleon is reported to have said, 'Give me English soldiers and French officers and I will conquer the world'. Possibly General Pétain, commanding the French Army south of the Somme, knew of this remark of Napoleon for on the evening of 24 March—that is, only three days after the German offensive commenced—he called on Clemenceau, the Premier of France, and discussed the grave situation with him. If Amiens fell, as seemed likely, Paris would be endangered. As a result of this information, reports Bean, Clemenceau said he 'was prepared to withdraw the machinery of government from Paris'. Pétain then hurried to the headquarters of Sir Douglas Haig, Commander-in-Chief of the British forces, to inform him of this and his alarm at the general situation. Haig, seeing the state of anxiety that Pétain was in and his agitation, started straight away to tell him his plans (which he had just imparted to General Byng, commander of the Third Army) to concentrate behind Byng all the reserves he could get. In the first place he was despatching from Flanders the five Australian divisions, the 3rd, 4th and 5th at once, to be followed later by the 1st and 2nd divisions as well as the New Zealand Division. By this means he was confident of stopping the enemy's advance on Amiens. He asked Pétain whether he would assemble as many divisions as he could to protect Byng's right flank. But Pétain, anxious for the safety of his own army and fearing that the debacle of the Fifth Army would affect his own troops, refused. Bean tells us that later Pétain told Clemenceau: 'The Germans will beat the British in the open field after which they will beat us too.'

Haig found that he was getting nowhere with Pétain in the matter of providing supporting troops, since Pétain said he feared a complete break-through by the Germans as the Fifth Army would not stand and fight. Haig therefore suddenly changed his thinking. Previously he had opposed any suggestion of a united army leader—a French Generalissimo —but now, realizing the necessity for it, he communicated with the War Cabinet and proposed such a move, offering to stand aside and suggesting that Foch become Generalissimo.*

This was agreed to and Foch took over at once, starting to push French reserves into the area south of the Somme.

---

* Ludendorff is said to have remarked that had he known that Foch would be made Generalissimo of the Allied Armies he would not have started his Spring Offensive.

Haig told Foch that the six divisions he was throwing in behind the Third Army—'the stalwart Australians'—would be enough to protect the line north of the Somme River. This they actually did; the 4th Brigade of the Australian 4th Division under Brigadier-General Brand arrived in time to prevent a break-through by advancing Germans at Hébuterne on the right of the Third Army, whilst the Australian 3rd Division filled the gap existing south of the 33rd British Division on the extreme left of the Fifth Army. Thus they drove the Germans back and made an advance of 2,000 yards, denying the Germans the use of the rising ground in front of Morlancourt. This was reported in the 1st Australian Division's daily intelligence report as a morale booster to the whole of the Third Army (but nothing was said about it in the British Army's daily intelligence report!)

The 5th Australian Division arrived on the Somme from Flanders on 5 April, took up defensive positions on the south bank of the Somme and prevented the Germans from occupying the heights overlooking the city of Amiens, a key strategical and tactical point covering Paris.

This division was placed under the command of the British III Corps (Lieutenant-General Butler). Two of these brigades filled the gap on the extreme left of the corps where the British 1st Cavalry Division was fighting an heroic rearguard action on a 5,000-yard front and being hard pressed. Outnumbered four or five times by crack German divisions, the 5th Division stood its ground and then, like the other Australian divisions, began driving the Germans back and recapturing the high ground opposite Villers-Bretonneux, which overlooked Amiens. As they advanced they disregarded the thousands of English troops fleeing in panic and then, having done their job, handed over to re-formed English regiments and retired to the rear to be ready again to counter-attack any fresh enemy breakthrough.

The 2nd Australian Division, arriving battalion by battalion, carried out a series of attacks and counter-attacks, further consolidating the defence of that part of the line.

Sir John Monash records that the Australians derived tremendous pride from finding themselves fighting in close association with famous British cavalry regiments. He demonstrates 'that this feeling was reciprocated' by quoting a letter written to him by Major-General Mullens, the officer commanding the 1st Cavalry Division.

> Thank you . . . for your most valuable and encouraging support and assistance, especially on the 30th March, when we had a hard fight to keep the Bosche out of our position. I was very much struck by the courtesy of yourself and your officers in coming to see me personally, and for your own and their keen desire to do everything in their power to help . . .
>
> Will you convey to all concerned my own appreciation and that of all ranks of the 1st Cavalry Division. It was a pleasure and an honour to be fighting alongside troops who displayed such magnificent *moral*. I only hope we may have the chance of co-operating with you again, and under more favourable circumstances.
>
> Yours sincerely,
(Sgnd.) R. L. MULLENS*

As each Australian division arrived from the north it had a brigade taken from it and placed as a reserve brigade to an English corps, ready as a counter-attacking force to cover any failure of the English divisions holding the line in front to stand firm when attacked.

Later, while the new Fourth Army that had superseded the Fifth Army was being formed, four Australian divisions for a time held, in front of Amiens, the whole of the front of the old Fifth Army, and on the right they made secure the gap on the left of the French Army, which made that front safe. It should be pointed out, however, that the Aus-

---

* John Monash, *The Australian Victories in France in 1918* (London, 1920), p. 32.

tralians were fortunate not to have been subjected to the first German onslaught at dawn on 21 March.

General Monash's claim that Australian troops retrieved the situation by holding up the German advance towards Amiens and Hazebrouck, and Foch's statement that Australians saved Paris and France are true inasmuch as in no case after the arrival of Australian troops on the threatened fronts did the Germans gain any more ground, but were forced out of tactical positions that they had won and then stopped their attacks. However, credit must be given to the magnificent defence by certain British divisions in holding the Germans for several days (notably the 9th and 35th Divisions) before the Australians arrived, and also the glorious resistance of the British Regular Cavalry, which diverted German attacks to the south of the Somme.

German records make it clear that in places they met with stubborn resistance and it is evident from these reports that the German offensives had been badly shaken before the arrival of the Australians. But undoubtedly the knowledge that they were about to be relieved by the Australians helped these British troops to hold on, particularly the 33rd and 55th Division. A major of the British Artillery fighting with the Fifth is quoted by Bean as saying that 'The Australians who came up near Hangard Wood were the first cheerful, stubborn people he had met in the retreat'.

Bean also records that the 'hard driven British troops and commanders who welcomed them on the actual battle-field' were impressed by 'the abounding willingness and virility of the [Australian] troops themselves, and the calibre of their officers'.

After fighting beside Brigadier Elliott and his men at Villers-Bretonneux and elsewhere, the Chestnut Troop of the Royal Horse Artillery commanded by Major van Straubenzee, D.S.O., repeating the courtesy extended by the Troop to two regiments of the Rifle Brigade in the Peninsular War, invited Elliott and the officers of his four battalions to be honorary members of their Mess as an open demonstration of their regard. Such feelings were equally entertained by Australians for all British Regulars of the Old Army that fought beside them in those operations.

When I was on leave in England I often heard it said by English officers, though not by those who had had experience of them, 'that Australians are wonderful in attack but not so good in defence owing to their poor discipline'. That there is no substance whatever in those statements is proved by the stubborn Australian resistance to the German counter-attacks at Pozières and Bullecourt in 1916-17, where they never lost a trench once captured, and by the performance of the 1st Division strung out on a 13,000-yard front at Lagnicourt.

General Haig at any rate did not hesitate to give the Australian troops the task of defending both Amiens and Hazebrouck during what remained of the German offensive, and he wrote to Birdwood* on 15 April that he needed 'reliable troops there', and that he was confident of the security of the area while the Australians held it.

General Plumer, the Army Commander Second Army, wrote that he wished the troops to be made aware of his appreciation of the work done by the division in the Strazeele Sector.

Yet at the time when Marshal Foch was saying to the Australians in Amiens Cathedral—7 November 1920—'You saved Amiens' and 'You saved France', hardly any word of appreciation was expressed by the British High Command or the English press. Again there was an official silence in the matter.

And in spite of his confidence in the Australians, General Haig, in reply to General Monash's protests about this silence, could only say that it had been 'for the sake of British morale'.

* G.O.C. The A.I.F.

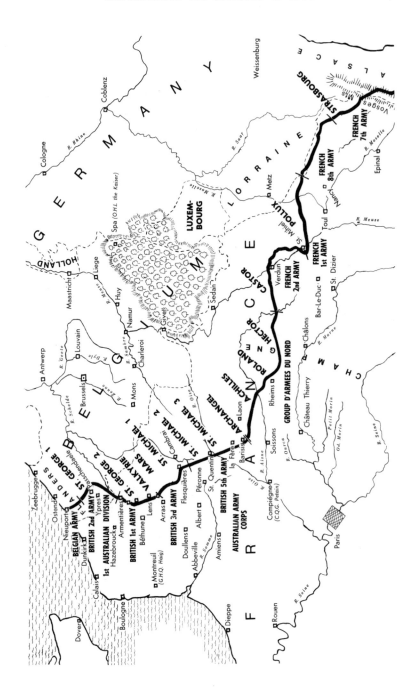

PART ONE

Summary of Australian Achievements— March, April and May 1918

The movement of the Australian 3rd and 4th Divisions from Flanders to the break in the line at the junction of the Third and Fifth British Armies, 26 March 1918. The arrow shows the movement of Australians.

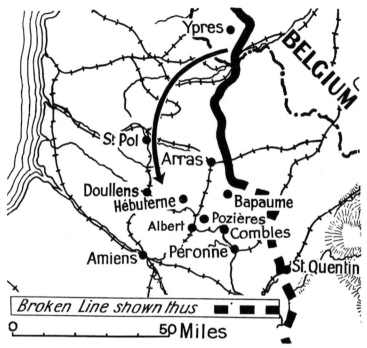

The arrow shows the movement of Australians.

Australian Divisions to the Rescue

March and April 1918

The 3rd Division of the Australian Corps, having received orders to proceed to the Somme area and come under command of the English X Corps, began entraining in the north at midnight on 25 March.

General Monash preceded the division by motor car and arrived, as ordered, in the area on the right of the Third Army on the following afternoon, to find the utmost confusion prevailing. Everything was in a state of chaos and he spent the next twenty-four hours endeavouring to find the headquarters of the X Corps. He sought them at various places only to discover that they had just left. Again and again he tracked them down, to find once more that they were no longer there. In desperation he sent off a despatch rider to Army Headquarters to say that he was without orders. In view of this he decided to make arrangements to cover the detrainment of his troops and to take up positions himself to make a stand, since all organizations of the X Corps had apparently broken down.

He established his headquarters in a small chateau at Couturelle where, fortunately, he found a telephone still working; the chateau's owner received him hospitably, providing him with a much-needed meal.

Shortly after this he learned of the presence in the neighbourhood of Major-General MacLagan, commanding the 4th Australian Division, which had also been ordered south. They met and together proceeded to work out a plan of co-ordinated action. The 4th Division had been on the move from the north by bus and route march for three days without rest. Major-General MacLagan had established a line of outposts in the supposed direction of the enemy, indicated by the steadily retreating mixed units and hundreds of civilian refugees with farm wagons packed high with household effects.

General Monash ultimately received orders by a despatch rider, and then by telephone, transferring his division from the X Corps to come under command of VII Corps on the Somme Front, commanded by Lt-General Congreve, V.C. General Monash wrote in his diary that this message, arriving when it did, saved him valuable time at a most critical juncture: had he not contacted General Congreve when he did, it is almost certain that his division would have arrived on the Somme too late to prevent the capture of Amiens.

At 10 o'clock at night, accompanied by four of his staff, he left Couturelle preceded by two motor cycle despatch riders and drove without lights through congested refugee traffic to Montigny. There he found General Congreve with his Chief of Staff in a deserted chateau by the roadside, seated at a small table examining a map by the flickering light of a candle.

To quote General Monash:

General Congreve was brief and to the point . . . 'At 4 o'clock today my Corps was holding a line from Albert to Bray when the line gave way. The enemy is now pushing westwards and if not stopped tomorrow will certainly secure all the heights overlooking Amiens. What you must try and do is to get your Division deployed across his path.' ... At that juncture General MacLagan arrived and received similar crisp orders to bring his Division into a position of support ... the [British] Fifth Army, south of the Somme, had practically melted away, while the French were also retiring ... leaving an hourly increasing gap between their north flank and the Somme.*

It was now 1 o'clock in the morning and Monash's division was twenty miles away. The situation called for 'quick decision and faultless executive action ... three large motor bus convoys could ... transport my Infantry during the night to the place appointed,' Monash stated. Working through the night till daybreak settling detailed arrangements, he and MacLagan then went their separate ways. Reports came that the enemy had entered Hébuterne, a very important tactical feature on the right of the Third Army, so MacLagan despatched his 4th Brigade there with instructions to recapture the village.

Fighting splendidly, two weak English divisions, the 42nd and 62nd, were barely holding on to the north of the village when the New Zealand Division, arriving battalion by battalion, filled the gap to the south of Hébuterne and started fighting as hard as that notable division could fight, attracting the full strength of the German attack in that sector.

How the 4th Brigade then brought to a standstill the German efforts to break through has already been told in the Introduction but that would have been impossible had not the New Zealanders closed the gap to the south and had not the help of the very tired 42nd and 62nd British Divisions been substantial. However, the value of the 4th Brigade's efforts at Hébuterne was fully acknowledged at the time by commanders on the spot, particularly by the British and New Zealanders beside whom they fought; and the fact that the IV Corps would not entrust Hébuterne to other avail-

* Monash, p. 27.

able troops is sufficient proof of the importance of the 4th Brigade's presence. The brigade remained under the orders of the 62nd British Division for over a month before it was released to return to its own division—the 4th Australian under MacLagan.

Defence of the Heights of Villers-Bretonneux overlooking Amiens

30 March to 5 April 1918

The situation opposite Villers-Bretonneux was pretty desperate when the 9th Brigade was detached from the 3rd Division and placed under the command of the 61st British Division. Rosenthal, the Australian Brigadier, was ordered to attack immediately. He placed Lt-Colonel Morshead in charge of the operation and told him to advance if possible to a depth of three and a half miles on a front of 2,700 yards. Bean reports the following: ' "When are we to do it?" asked Morshead. "Now." "Any artillery?" "No." "Do you know where the British Line is?" "No." "Can I have some troops to support me?" "Yes, the 34th." ... Rosenthal told Morshead not to use the 34th if he could avoid doing so.'

As Morshead was instructing his company commanders a junior British cavalry officer rode up and said he was Lieut. Barron of the 12th Lancers, and that they had been ordered to help the Australians in their advance by supporting their northern flank.

Lt-Colonel Morshead (later the famous commander of the 9th Division A.I.F. on the Western Desert in World War II and the hero of the battle of El Alamein) wrote in his diary of this action: 'It was a proud moment and a privilege for me to work with such a fine regiment as the 12th Lancers.' Their orderly approach march instilled in his men (of the 34th Battalion) the utmost enthusiasm and this example of a

19

British Regular regiment went a long way to neutralize the bad showing of the English infantry regiments, which were fleeing in disorder. As the 33rd Battalion moved to the attack, almost all British troops whom they encountered were coming back in the opposite direction and shouting that the enemy was in overwhelming strength.

Five junior English officers were found alone, lying in a hollow covered by a waterproof sheet. When asked where their men were, one pointed nonchalantly with his finger and said 'Over there somewhere.' 'Well, what about seeing what you can do by gathering in stragglers and making a stand,' an Australian officer said. After some persuasion they reluctantly agreed to do so, but showed no enthusiasm.

But the Lancers were of the 'old school'. They drove back the advancing Germans on the flanks and allowed the Australians to assemble for the attack, which was carried out with great enthusiasm. Losses were severe—8 officers and 1,600 o/ranks. The British line was enormously wide, with only about 300 men holding—with wide gaps—a front of nearly a mile. In this operation the full task of the Australians was not achieved but it was understood that part of the intention of the British Command was for the Australians to increase the confidence of the British troops as well as to diminish that of the enemy, and this objective was certainly reached. A young officer of the Lancers attached for the operation to Colonel Morshead's staff begged permission to lead a cavalry charge—such was the cavalry's spirit—but Morshead withheld his consent.

Morshead wrote in his diary: 'All ranks (of the cavalry) were eager to give every possible help ... was able too, to judge of the splendid work they are doing for the army at the present time, and cannot be too highly praised.'

The Australians were relieved by the 10th Essex and other troops of the 18th Division, then marched back to resume their role as counter-attacking troops when called upon.

Recapture of Villers-Bretonneux
25 April 1918

The English garrison that had taken over the defence of Villers-Bretonneux put up a very poor resistance when attacked, and once more Villers-Bretonneux was in the enemy's hands. In the meantime, so sure was General 'Pompey' Elliott, commanding the 15th Australian Brigade, which had gone into reserve, that this would happen that he already had plans for a counter-attack to recapture the heights. He offered to carry these out but the British corps commander to whom he was attached withheld permission.

As soon as it was clear that Villers-Bretonneux was lost General Foch's Headquarters showered down orders for its immediate recapture.

General Rawlinson, commanding the new Fourth Army, had already taken measures to do this and ordered the nearest Australian reserve brigade, the 13th of the 4th Division billeted at Querrieu, north of the Somme, to route march at once to III Corps Headquarters (a day's march away) to assist in its recapture, which was imperative for the security of Amiens. The Australian 5th Division was also instructed to help the 8th British Division in an attack, but it never eventuated. Elliott, whose 15th Australian Brigade was on the left of the 5th Australian Division and nearest to the British 8th Division, was itching to counter-attack himself and, as previously mentioned, had offered help to

Lt. General Butler commanding III Corps, for which he had been snubbed.

When the 13th Australian Brigade arrived, sent for by Rawlinson, he allotted it to his 8th Division under Major-General Heneker.

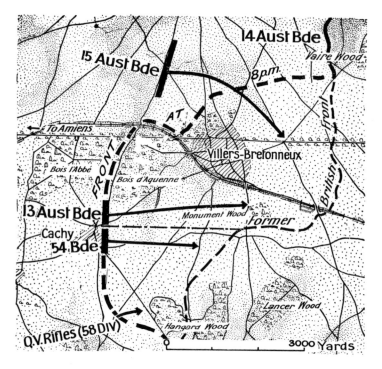

In the meantime, Brigadier-General Glasgow, commander of the Australian 13th Brigade, who had been lent a car by General Monash, reached Corps Headquarters ahead of his brigade. He immediately went into conference with Major-General Heneker, who informed him of the plans made for the counter-attack. Glasgow then went on a personal re-connaissance to view the ground over which he was to attack. When he returned he informed Heneker that he intended to start the attack from a north-south line and attack eastwards and past the south of Villers-Bretonneux. Bean records their conversation:

> 'But you can't do that,' was the reply, 'the corps commander says the attack is to be made from Cachy.' Glasgow said he could not do it that way. 'Why it's against all the teaching of your own army, Sir, to attack across the enemy's front. They'd get hell from the right . . . Tell us what you want us to do, Sir,' he said 'but you must let us do it our own way.'

After some argument he won his point. But when Glasgow asked Heneker the planned time of the operation and was told that the corps commander 'wished it done at 8', he retorted 'If it was God Almighty who gave the order we couldn't do it in daylight'. Glasgow, however, eventually compromised by agreeing to start the attack at 10 o'clock, half an hour earlier than his preference, 10.30.

Brigadier-General Elliott, of the 15th Australian Brigade, had reported to Major-General Heneker earlier in the afternoon and won permission to carry out his portion of the attack in accordance with the scheme that he had planned so enthusiastically and had wished to carry out earlier: he was certain that the British troops defending Villers-Bretonneux would panic when attacked and was ready for this contingency. Glasgow, arriving at his headquarters about 8 o'clock, was enthusiastically received by Elliott, who was heartened by the knowledge that he would have Glasgow's brigade on his right instead of the English brigade as previously planned. Together they made some alterations to Elliott's plan and then Glasgow hurried away to a conference with his battalion commanders.

It was then 4 o'clock and Glasgow asked for a car to send for his four battalion commanders to meet him. He issued them with a map each and explained that he would attack eastwards on the south side of the village with two battalions in line and one following close behind. They were to ignore the wood and the village. His 51st Battalion was to advance 4,000 yards and then turn left and join up with Elliott's 15th Brigade, which was to attack on the northern side of Villers-Bretonneux.

The attack was to take place in pitch darkness and direction had to be maintained—a difficult task to undertake. Much explaining had to be done by the company commanders to their platoon commanders, who in turn had to tell their men, as they were still several miles away from their 'start line', and time was short.

The 52nd Battalion was to advance on the right of the 51st, dropping its companies as it advanced, to protect the flanks of the leading battalions. The 3rd Battalion in the brigade was to advance and stop after going 1,000 yards. As it would be dark, white tape lines had to be laid just before zero hour to mark the boundaries on the start line and enable the companies to form up facing their objective. Two English battalions would attack from the north side and would mop up the village after it was surrounded.

By the time Glasgow's conference with his battalion commanders was over it was after 7 o'clock, only three hours to go before the attack was to take place and much still to be done. None of the troops had seen the country they were to fight over and there were few prominent features. The colonels of the two leading battalions were to keep in close touch with each other and to meet at four points during the advance.

Glasgow then proceeded to establish his headquarters alongside Elliott so that the two brigadiers could also be closely in touch with each other throughout the operation. They were to arrange to meet each other at crucial points.

Days before, Elliott had directed his battalion commanders to be prepared to carry out the counter-attack planned by him, and all that was now necessary was to bring the plan up-to-date. But this proved difficult to do in the time avail-

Villers-Bretonneux, from the south. Advancing from the other side of the town, the 15th Brigade first met enemy opposition near the wood seen in the centre. (The trenches in the foreground were dug later.) *Source:* A.W.M.

The Brigadiers chiefly responsible for the counterattack at the second battle of Villers - Bretonneux: *(above)* Brigadier-General William Glasgow, 13th Brigade, who is seen at the extreme left of the picture and *(left)* Brigadier-General H. E. Elliott, 15th Brigade. *Source:* A.W.M.

Officers of the 8th Battalion, photographed just before the German Spring Offensive in March 1918. Included are from left: *(front row)* Capt. Campbell, Capt. Blackman, Lieut Fenton, Major Eller, Lt-Col. Mitchell, Major Traill, Lieut Temple, Capt. Freeman. *(2nd row)* Lieuts Andrewarthur, Bourke, Wales, Perkins, Foote, Joynt, Hudson, ———, Young, ———, Claridge. *(3rd row)* Lieuts Finlayson, S. Young, Pitt, Tickell, Dowling, Woodhouse, Evans, Anderson. *Source:* A.W.M.

Just out of the Line at Wyshaetyte Ridge, where they had spent Christmas 1917, officers and sergeants of D coy, 8th Battalion. Capt. Alex Campbell is seated third from the left. *Source:* A.W.M.,

Colonel Herod and Officers of the 7th Battalion who, detraining before the 8th Battalion, moved out and took up a line of outposts on a three-mile front to cover the deployment of the remainder of the 1st Australian Division. *Source:* A.W.M.

able. The advent of Glasgow's brigade operating on the right instead of the English brigade made changes in the direction of attack by two of Elliott's battalions necessary, and in the short time available for the new plans to be explained to the troops concerned, some difficulties were experienced before the 15th Brigade was ready to attack. Consequently at 10 o'clock, when Glasgow's 13th Brigade commenced their attack the 15th Brigade was still only forming up. Some confusion resulted from the 15th Brigade's attack failing to coincide with that of Glasgow's brigade but in some degree this turned out to be of advantage as the attention of the Germans was directed to their left flank, where they were heavily engaged with the 13th Brigade's advance, and Elliott's men were able to advance at first without much opposition.

At 10 o'clock a huge bombardment of gas shells fell on Elliott's men as they were moving up; gas masks had to be put on and in the semi-darkness orientation was difficult. Consequently their attack did not get away until 12 o'clock, two hours behind scheduled time, but when they did get going observers wrote that there was never anything like it in the whole of the war. The men of the 15th Brigade charged forward, shouting, cheering and yelling so as to keep in touch with each other. They charged into the night and the enemy in panic fled before them. Others rushed out of their dugouts with their hands up, shouting 'Kamerad'. Isolated bodies of Germans manned their machine-guns and put up a fight until they were bayoneted or shot.

By 4 o'clock next morning, on Anzac Day, 25 April, the third anniversary of the landing on Gallipoli, the two Australian brigades had established themselves on a line completely cutting off the town of Villers-Bretonneux, but a bit short of their objective. This was because the 13th Brigade battalions got mixed up when in the dark they came up against the wire entanglements constructed by the British in front of the village to aid its defence. Suffering heavy casualties and unable to find breaks in the wire, they could go no further.

Earlier in their attack there were many acts of extreme bravery. The Germans saw the attacking troops approaching and fired hundreds of flares, making the scene as bright as day. They opened fire, sweeping the ground to the front with intense machine-gun fire, particularly from the wood on their left. It looked as if the advance might be permanently held up.

Before the attack took place Glasgow had requested that an English brigade should clear the Germans from the wood on the left of Villers-Bretonneux, realizing the great danger it would be to his left flank by enfilade fire. He got a report that this had been done and that the wood was now occupied by British troops. Glasgow's battalion commanders were informed of this and in turn told their men not to worry if they saw movement in the wood—it would only be the Tommies mopping up any Germans still there. Consequently, the right of the attacking troops believed there was no danger from their left, when in actual fact they were all in a precarious position.

The following account draws heavily on the Australian War Memorial publication *They Dared Mightily,* which describes deeds that won the V.C.

The leading platoons on the extreme left of the attack, when fired on from the wood, went to ground and lay there under the glare of the flares. A platoon sergeant of the platoon next but one from the wood crept up to the commander of the platoon on the extreme left, Lieutenant C. W. K. Sadlier, a West Australian, and asked him what he was going to do.

'Carry out the order, go straight to our objective,' replied Sadlier.

'You can't do it,' said Stokes the sergeant, 'we'll all be killed.'

'Well what else can we do, we must help the advance?'

'Let's collect our bombers and go into the wood and bomb those guns out.'

It looked certain death to attempt this, but it seemed the only thing to do. Sadlier sent his runner to warn his company commander that his platoon would clear the wood but all he could find where the company headquarters should have been, were dead men. Sadlier then went to the support company following close behind and asked the officer in command to push on and take up the gap that would be left in the main line when he withdrew his platoons to storm the wood. Returning to his platoon, he got his Lewis gunner to open fire on the German machine-gun in the wood immediately to his front, and at the same time got his bombers into action. Then with the rest of his platoon he rushed that part of the wood. It was a bold thing to do but it succeeded. The Germans were caught unawares and before they could act, Sadlier, Stokes and their men were amongst them, firing in the dark in amongst the trees and around bushes, stumbling into German posts and using their bayonets. Finding a bag of German bombs, they threw them at the surprised Germans as they rushed to occupy their posts. The Germans resisted bravely until overcome. In the first post attacked, a German who held up his hands crying '*Kamerad*' shot Sadlier in the thigh, but Sadlier still carried on until wounded a second time, when he had to go to the rear. Sgt Stokes then took command and carried on, the two platoons continuing to mop up German posts. By means of the audacious attacks all the German machine guns along the edge of the Wood were eventually silenced and this great danger to the advancing 13th Brigade was removed. Sadlier and Stokes were both recommended for the Victoria Cross, so richly deserved, but the award was given to Sadlier in recognition of the bravery of the whole force, which had shown extraordinary dash.

In the granting of the V.C. to Sadlier, standard practice was followed in that bravery alone does not justify the award, but 'the carrying out of an act of extreme bravery, the effect of which enables a victory to be won and the subsequent saving of casualties.' By subduing the enemy enfilade fire directed at the left flank of the attacking force Sadlier's act undoubtedly enabled the attacking brigade to continue its advance and ultimately reach its objective of encircling the town of Villers-Bretonneux.

After Villers-Bretonneux was surrounded, both Generals Glasgow and Elliott complained to the corps commander that the English battalions had not advanced as arranged and that, as there was no mopping-up done, both Australian brigades had suffered. However, it was found later that the English battalions did attack but could make no progress. They ran up against strong resistance and suffered heavy casualties, just as Glasgow foresaw would happen if his brigade had made a frontal attack from the north as originally ordered. One of the English battalions lost about 450 men, over half its strength, including its commander.

The total Australian casualties for the recapture of Villers-Bretonneux amounted to 2,473. Out of this number the 13th Brigade lost 1,009 and the 15th Brigade 455. The 51st Battalion alone lost 365 officers and men. Although these Australian casualties were severe, the value of the result was out of all proportion to them. Throughout the operation of the defence and later counter-attacks, the 8th British Division lost 3,500 men, the 18th Division 2,500 and the 58th Division 3,600—at total of 9,600 all ranks, including prisoners lost.

Had General Glasgow insisted on his own proposal to attack at 10.30 p.m. the success of the operation would probably have been greater than it was.

The German 77th Reserve Division lost nearly 3,000 men and the 4th Guard Division 2,000. Altogether the Germans lost 8,000.

The two Australian brigadiers who were under Major-General Heneker's orders for this operation were men of quite outstanding strength and their forcefulness was not wholly relished by Heneker. Amid all the telegrams of congratulation that afterwards reached the two brigades, there came no message from the divisional commander to whom they had been lent. However, two senior members of the British 8th Division staff rode over and thanked Glasgow for his brigade's effort and one of the brigade commanders of General Heneker's division, Brigadier-General Grogan of the 23rd British Brigade, who was in a good position to know the nature of the achievement, generously described it as 'Perhaps the greatest individual feat of the war . . . a military epic'.

A historian's account of the operation covering the recapture of Villers-Bretonneux

Gregory Blaxland's book *Amiens: 1918* gives an account of the operation based on the official account covering the recapture of Villers-Bretonneux. It is a shocking case of misrepresentation on the part of Army Command—the report, obviously compiled after the event, claims that the credit for originating the plan of attack belongs to General Rawlinson. The account given is a jumble of the two plans, Glasgow's and Rawlinson's. It reads:

> Rawlinson's reaction to the crisis was to demand that Villers-Bretonneux be retaken at once . . . he resolved on a night attack to be launched as a pincer movement by his Army reserve, the 13th Australian Brigade, and a brigade from the division on the right of the Australian line, the

5th Division ... On the right of the pincer a composite
brigade of III Corps was to enlarge the frontage of the
attack ... At 2 p.m. Rawlinson rang Butler [III Corps
Commander] and explained exactly how the attack was to
be carried out ... Rawlinson sent one of his staff officers
to remain with him [Butler] and make sure that there was
no alteration to his (Rawlinson's) orders.

Haig arrived and approved the plans, and at 3.45 there
was a visit from Foch's envoy ...The plan was daring. The
two Australian brigades had to advance two miles in the
moonlight, on either side of Villers-Bretonneux, with
their inner flanks exposed to enfilade fire; there was little
information as to where the enemy was and little time for
assembly ...*

It is obvious that the plan as carried out was not Rawlinson's
at all. The one claimed as his (and said to be approved by
Haig) was made before 2 p.m. At that time Glasgow was
doing a reconnaissance and had not yet submitted his plan to
III Corps, so the plan submitted and approved by Haig must
have been the one that Rawlinson said *'must not be altered'*
and sent his staff officer to keep intact!

* Gregory Blaxland, *Amiens: 1918* (London, 1968), pp. 128, 129.

The 4th Australian Division fills the gap on the right of the Third Army

April 1918

Important in all as the operation of recapturing Villers-Bretonneux was, the earlier work of the other two brigades of the 4th Division on the north of the Somme at Dernancourt, whilst not so spectacular, was a much greater military achievement—described by Bean as 'the strongest [enemy attack] ever met [and defeated] by Australian troops, and, by reason of the tactical position, one of the most difficult to resist'. Bean also wrote that 'this stubborn fight left the Australians overflowing with confidence, the Germans bitterly depressed'. For the Australians had resisted and defeated a most bitter attack by the 50th Prussian Reserve Division (supported by other divisions), which had achieved their plan of placing themselves in rear of the 12th Australian Brigade's front line and getting into position for a further advance towards Amiens. They had outflanked the 47th and 48th Australian Battalions, which in their turn had to extricate themselves from a most dangerous position—a feat they nevertheless managed with great efficiency.

The other battalions of the two brigades of the 4th Division beat off attack after attack although disadvantageously placed tactically; and they were without the help of their machine gun battalion owing to dense fog, which prevented effective sweeping machine gun fire through inability to see the targets.

31

The eight battalions, little more than half-strength, and numbering in all fewer than 3,000 men, beat off and defeated two and a half German divisions (about 25,000 men). The 48th, with portion of the 47th Battalion, repelled the greater part of the German attack, standing firm in their post and resisting all German attempts to overwhelm them. A few month later some men of the 48th Battalion found that the Germans had paid their own tribute by inscribing on a couple of crosses the words: 'Here lies a brave English soldier'.

Further Battles in Defence of Amiens

April-May 1918

The British Second Battle of Villers-Bretonneux captured the town but the Germans were still in strong positions on the south and east at Monument Wood and Hanguard.

A brand new Moroccan Division attacked across the open in daylight (a night attack to those reckless troops was unthinkable). It was only partly successful and the cost was tremendous. The division failed to reach all its objectives and there were 3,500 casualties.

The III Corps Commander then ordered a combined attacked on Monument Wood by British and Australian divisions.

The losses in this attack were also very heavy, the 60th Australian Battalion losing more men than in the main attack on Villers-Bretonneux itself. However, as was often said, the Australian gains were out of all proportion to their losses.

The defence of Amiens now being much more secure, General Haig, in order to ensure a firm junction with the French, ordered the III Corps to change over and move to the left. All the Australian brigades were then gathered in under their own divisions and again formed the Australian Corps, which was placed on the extreme right of the British line next to the French.

In spite of their losses the troops were bursting with confidence. They had done more than their share in saving Amiens but, owing to their casualties and the lack of reinforcements, three battalions that had become famous, the 36th, 47th and 52nd, were disbanded to maintain their sister units.

'Silence is Golden'

So much for some of the outstandingly successful operations conducted by the A.I.F. divisions when the Fifth Army 'broke' in March and April 1918.

But hardly a word of these great achievements was allowed to leak out, nor was any public recognition made by British Army Headquarters.

However, credit must be given to many acts of gallantry by the British, both of individuals and units. When it is considered that the Fifth Army of twenty divisions (eighteen Infantry and two Cavalry) was attacked by the bulk of about forty-four German divisions, supported by another forty in reserve, there must have been a lot of glory shown, as well as shame, in the defence. But very little has been told about it. The reaction of the High Command seems to have been: 'Silence is Golden' — particularly as to the work of the A.I.F.

There was one notable exception, an article by Philip Gibbs in the *Daily Telegraph*, which Monash called 'the first public avowal' of the brilliant episode of the recapture of Villers-Bretonneux on 2 May.

General Monash also wrote the following to his wife:

The question of the adequate recognition of the work done in the war by Australian troops, and indeed by all

35

Dominion troops of the Empire, is a very burning one. Far from it being the case that Dominion troops have in the past received more than their fair share of recognition, the exact contrary is the case ... The Imperial Government and also G.H.Q. have been rather afraid of the effect of such propaganda, and they have rather erred on the side of unduly suppressing references to the deeds of the Australians. In connection with the present counter-offensive the London Press started very badly, and, in fact, in several striking instances attributed successes achieved by the Australians to other troops who had previously failed in the same tasks. I made a very serious remonstration about this to Perry Robinson of *The Times,* to Rawlinson, to Lawrence, and to the Chief of the Imperial General Staff, Sir Henry Wilson, telling them plainly that my one appeal to my troops was the prestige of Australian arms, and that, unless the performances of the Australians were justly placarded, I would not hold myself responsible for the maintenance of their fighting spirit ... These remonstrations have had an astonishingly successful result, because a complete change has come over the scene, and, as you will see by the very large number of cuttings I have recently sent you, the London Press has latterly given us quite generous recognition.*

A German war correspondent wrote: 'the Australians and Canadians are much the best troops that the English have', a statement taken by British General Headquarters as merely an attempt to create jealousy between the Mother Country and the dominions.

This it undoubtedly did. And this jealousy gathered weight as the war went on and remained with certain members of the High Command and the War Office until long after the Armistice and, unfortunately, still exists in some quarters.

---

* F. M. Cutlack (ed.), *War Letters of General Monash (Sydney, 1934)*, pp. 267-8.

Saving the Channel Ports: the Defence of Hazebrouck in Flanders by the 1st Australian Division

10-25 April 1918

The Germans, having failed to break through on the Somme, now turned their attention to their second planned offensive in Flanders, which they originally called 'George'. This was to attack the British Second Army on the sector held by the Portuguese. The plan was aimed at capturing the Channel Ports of Calais, Boulogne and Le Havre and then driving down behind Paris. In February Ludendorff postponed this plan for the grand offensive to take place on the Somme, which was called 'Michael'. 'Georgette', as 'George' was now renamed, was kept as an alternative plan to destroy the British Army if the Somme offensive failed. The Germans were well prepared for this second grand drive: huge supplies and stocks of war material had been stored behind Armentières in Flanders during the late months of winter.

The British Line, with the exception of the 5th and 9th Divisions on the northern sector of the front, was held by two Portuguese divisions and the tired British divisions, late of the Fifth Army, which had relieved the Australians and New Zealanders when they were sent down to the Somme. These divisions had been re-formed and brought up to strength by drafts of inexperienced reinforcements who had never been in action; some had not even fired a rifle or Lewis gun.

The two Portuguese divisions were in a state of semi-mutiny, had no interest whatsoever in the war, and were known to be untrustworthy if attacked. Arrangements had been made for their withdrawal from the Line and replacement by a British division, actually on the day before the Germans attacked, but the relieving English division had asked to be given another day to complete their preparations for the relief. When the Germans attacked, the Portuguese panicked and fled—some of them did not stop running until they reached the coast. The Germans poured through the gap left in the line, penetrating ten miles on a four-mile front and outflanking two good British divisions. The 9th British Division, which included the 4th Guards Brigade, a South African Brigade and a Scottish one, put up a tremendous fight and fought rearguard actions for several days, ultimately falling back on the 1st Australian Division which had come up from the Somme. The Australians had just arrived at the Somme to relieve their 3rd Division opposite Morlancourt when they received the order to return to Flanders.

The Commander-in-Chief of the British Army, Field Marshal Sir Douglas Haig, personally gave the direct order for the 1st Australian Division to 'about turn' and entrain for the north, although General de Lisle of the British V Corps claims to have been the first to suggest it. However, Sir Douglas Haig maintained that it was his own idea to send for the 1st Australian Division. Be that as it may, it has been said that the events that followed included one of the most dramatic incidents in the history of the A.I.F.

Very little, if any, reference is made in British war history books or newspaper reports about the work of the 1st Australian Division at this time, or since, but Bean says that probably only the British High Command fully realized just how critical the situation was at that time—'the British Army was practically at the end of its reserves'.

Sir Douglas Haig himself had written his famous 'Backs to the Wall' appeal to all troops of the B.E.F:

> There is no other course open to us but to fight it out! Every position must be held to the last man: there must be no retirement. With our backs to the wall, and believing in the justice of our cause, each one of us must fight on to the end. The safety of our Homes and the Freedom of mankind alike depend upon the conduct of each one of us at this critical moment.

Haig has been criticized by many English writers for what they call his 'panic alarmism' in issuing that challenge. 'He should have known better', wrote one historian. 'It was so un-English of him and so unwarranted', wrote another. One historian makes one of his characters ask, 'What ruddy wall?' A Tommy is made to ridicule the idea. A senior commander is reported as refusing to allow the 'Order' to be read to his troops; a battalion commander destroys it. But had any one of those writers been on the spot at the time they might have held very different views on the subject. As with the Fifth Army on the Somme, all resistance to the enemy had broken down except for some isolated units which were fighting bravely. It was probably to these comparatively few troops that Haig addressed his words.

As Bean says, 'The crisis was due to the simple fact that the British divisions which had been holding the Germans on or near the Lys . . . could hold them no longer'. Hence the sending for the 1st Australian Division.

That part of the British Line had collapsed. Hazebrouck, a town similar to Amiens on the Somme in its tactical and strategical importance, was being threatened.

On receiving Haig's orders, the 1st Division turned round and, marching all night, arrived at Amiens Station to find that the railway yards had been bombed. There was a four-hour delay while an important railway bridge was repaired and the railway civilian staff returned to their jobs after fleeing from the station during the bombing. The bombing had caused the 7th Australian Battalion, which preceded the 8th Battalion, to lose a lot of its transport vehicles in the station yards whilst it was entraining. They arrived at Hazebrouck in the late afternoon, immediately moved out seven miles and threw out a screen to cover the detraining of the 8th Battalion and the other battalions of the 1st Division which were following on the next trains.

The Chief of Staff of the Second Army, Major-General C. Harington, was waiting on the station to receive the 8th Battalion. The Officer's Call was blown and he briefly addressed them. The position was very critical, he said. The five divisions out in front were no longer holding the enemy and all communications had broken down. He added the words: 'the 1st Australian Division is the only formed body of troops now between here and the Channel Ports'. The atmosphere was tense and the general feeling was one of hopelessness—what could two half-strength battalions and a machine gun company (all that had arrived at the time) do to oppose as many as five German divisions advancing victoriously towards them?

But the 1st Australian Division did hold the oncoming Germans, as their 3rd, 4th and 5th brother-divisions held the Germans on the Somme and saved Amiens.

In his book on Plumer, the G.O.C. Second Army to whom he was Chief of Staff, Harington described the scene on Hazebrouck railway station as the 8th Battalion started to detrain. He was most enthusiastic at their bearing as they marched away from the station: 'Glorious Fellows!' he wrote.

They marched through the night with scouts out in front and at daybreak took up a defensive line in front of Nieppe Forest, one weak platoon post of twenty-five men to every 300 yards, and there they stood their ground as the remnants of four British divisions retreated (or rather, fled) through them.

The 1st Australian Division saved Hazebrouck, an important railway centre, which meant that the Channel Ports also were saved. In the course of the next three months the Huns never gained another foot of ground in that area. During that time the 1st Division engaged and defeated nine German divisions and yet, just as on the Somme, there was never a public word of recognition—it was again a case of 'a conspiracy of silence'. Many books have been written about the defence of Hazebrouck and the battle of the Lys, but with hardly a word about the 1st Australian Division except the repeated assertion that the Australians had come but were four hours late. Even Churchill, who eulogizes 'the glorious defence of Hazebrouck' by the English divisions concerned merely remarks on the lateness of the Australians.

I must exclude from this criticism Gregory Blaxland, and his book *Amiens: 1918*. This writer describes the arrival of the Australians on Hazebrouck station and refers to the 1st Australian Division as playing the 'saviour's rôle'.* He is also generous in his account of the work of the other Australian divisions down on the Somme.

To a lesser degree Barrie Pitt, in *1918—the Last Act,* may be defended. But he too repeats the story about the Australians being four hours late. However, he gives a reason (unlike most other writers)—'congestion on the railways'.† He also gives a fairly detailed account of the A.I.F.'s part in the Battle of the Somme and Germany's 'Black Day'.

However, when the time came for the 1st Australian Division to leave the Second Army and return to the Anzac Corps, General Plumer gathered some of the senior members of the Division together and told them that perhaps 'no division . . . in the whole British Army' had 'done more to destroy the morale of the enemy than the 1st Australian Division'.

---

* Blaxland, p. 123.
† Barrie Pitt, *1918—the Last Act* (London, 1962), p. 121.

'Peaceful Penetration'

When both German offensives failed and active warfare by the Germans died down, trench warfare was resumed. On both fronts held by the Australians, however, on the Somme and in Flanders, there was no respite—although things were absolutely dormant on those fronts held by English divisions. Opposite the Australian lines a constant form of warfare called 'peaceful penetration' was carried out.

For the next three or four months there was hardly a day in which some sort of quiet penetration of the German lines was not carried out. It took the form of individual raids on the enemy posts opposite the Australians—in which prisoners were captured and brought in until a complete moral ascendancy over the Germans was obtained.

An official historian wrote: 'The full value of the Anzac aggressive defence during the four months of "peaceful penetration" was not generally known in the B.E.F. or by the English public whose general opinion was that they [the Australians] were getting too much credit'. But G.H.Q. and the headquarters of the Armies concerned were fully aware of the facts. The neighbouring 9th Division's commander wrote: 'During the last two months we have admired the successful activity of the Australian troops in defence.' The history of the 29th Division (also alongside the Australians) states that the 1st Australian Division set them a splendid example.

It was four months before the 1st Division was allowed to rejoin the Australian Corps. At every request by General Monash for its return he was told that the Australians were indispensable, and the only reliable Division covering the Channel Ports.

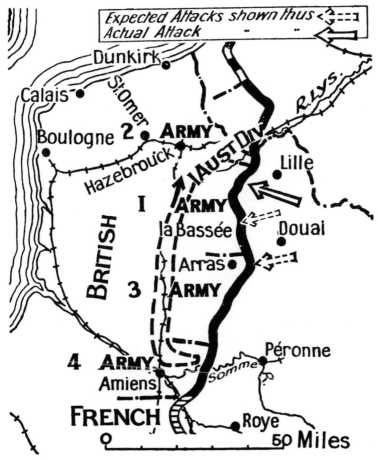

'Backs to the wall!'—the journey down to the Somme and back to Flanders of the 1st Australian Division

When the time did come—at the beginning of August 1918—for the 1st Australian Division to leave the Second Army many tributes were paid by local commanders for the work done in the saving of Hazebrouck.

The following is a letter received from the Corps Commander XV Corps, Lt-General Beavoir de Lisle, the contents of which the divisional commander wished to be conveyed to the troops at the earliest opportunity:

To

Major-General T. W. GLASGOW, C.B., C.M.G., D.S.O., Commanding 1st Australian Division.

Before your magnificent Division leaves my Corps, I wish to thank you and all ranks under your command for the exceptional services rendered during the past four months.

Joining the Corps on April 12th, during the Battle of the LYS, the Division selected and prepared a position to defend the HAZEBROUCK Front, and a few days later, repulsed two heavy attacks, with severe losses to the enemy. This action brought the enemy's advance to a standstill.

Since then, the Division has held the most important Sector of the Front continuously, and by skilful raiding and minor operations, has advanced the line over a mile on a Front of 5,000 yards, capturing just short of 1,000 prisoners, and causing such damage to the Troops of the enemy that nine divisions have been replaced.

The complete success of all minor operations, the skill displayed by the patrols by day as well as by night, the gallantry and determination of the troops, and their high state of training and discipline, have excited the admiration and emulation of all, and I desire that you will convey to all ranks my high appreciation of their fine work and my regret that the Division is leaving my Command.

(Sgd.) Beavoir de Lisle
Lieutenant-General
Commanding XV Corps.

XV Corps Headquarters
4th August, 1918.

PART TWO

The Author's Diary, covering the period January to August 1918

'. . . a narrative most fortunately provided by an officer of the 8th Battalion, Lieutenant Joynt, which gives the most vivid and accurate picture of the situation at this time, so far as the 1st [Australian] Division was concerned in it.'

(C. E. W. Bean)

Diary Synopsis

January to March 1918	Preparations being made to prepare defences to counteract the expected German offensive in the spring (March and April 1918).
21 March	The Great German Offensive on the Somme.
	The work of the A.I.F. in helping to bring about its repulse.
7 April to May	Saving the Channel Ports— the defence of Hazebrouck by the 1st Australian Division.
	General Monash's appointment as G.O.C. the Australian Corps.
	The Battle of Hamel.
June to July	'Peaceful Penetration' by the Australian divisions on all fronts held by the A.I.F.
8 August to 26 August	Germany's 'Black Days'—the combined Dominion Forces offensive (Canadian and Australian and the British 3rd Corps supporting on their flanks), August 1918, leading to the Armistice ten weeks later.
21 August to 5 October	Events leading up to the Armistice on 11 November 1918.

It was my practice after every 'stunt' and tour in the Line to immediately write up an account of what happened whilst things were still fresh in my mind. This I did, no matter how tired I felt, because I realized that it would form a valuable record. I later deposited the original diaries with the Australian War Museum authorities, who, in due course forwarded me typewritten copies; and it is these copies that I have used in writing this book.

In a few instances I have filled in gaps, but in no case have I altered the text as written at the time. Nor has the editor's hand been permitted to tamper with this section of the book, except for a few spelling corrections.

Important incidents that I was unaware of at the time, and which help the history, I have covered in my 'Postscripts'.

Christmas Festivities

During December 1917 and January 1918 the 1st Division, along with the other Australian Divisions, held the line along the Messines Wytschaete Ridge. Snow covered the ground and the earth was frozen a foot or more deep.

In view of the anticipated German offensive in the Spring, now that their Eastern Army was no longer fighting (following the Russian Revolution of October 1917), the main task of the British Army was building defences covering the approaches to the Channel Ports and Amiens. Each battalion in the front line appointed a Works Officer. I was handed that job for the 8th Battalion and spent the next month in supervising the erection of barbed wire entanglements in front of our outpost positions following a design approved by Battalion Headquarters.

The Reserve company of the battalion provided the working party of about fifty men who reported to me at a selected spot every evening after dark. It was interesting work and I

enjoyed the job. Having strung a line of 'apron' wire immediately in front of our entrenched posts I began to run a
second line about a hundred yards further out into No Man's
Land. We worked by the light of the German flares which
Fritz continuously kept firing. On the contrary, we only used
flares when it was absolutely necessary.

I was out with two or three men trying to establish how
far the Hun's own outposts extended towards our line when
we perceived a party of Germans creeping towards our lines.
We kept perfectly still and the Huns crawled past us as we
lay on the ground, only a few yards away. We could see they
intended carrying out a raid—there was a German officer
at each end of the group of about twenty men.

As soon as the Germans passed us we rose up and dashed
for our own lines skirting our own outpost line. While we
were doing this the Huns surrounded and captured one of
our advanced 'listening posts' of four men and a Lewis gun,
having shot the lookout man first. We reached one of our
forward posts ahead of this happening as we were running
whereas the Huns were crawling. We gave the alarm and
2nd/Lieut. P. Lay, the post commander gathered a dozen
men and without a minute's hesitation rushed out and
making a detour, overtook the Huns returning with their
captives by getting between them and their own lines, taking
the Germans completely by surprise. They killed eleven of
the Huns and captured the remainder including two German
officers and released three of our own men (that had been
captured in the post). None of the German raiding party
got back to their own lines—a truly magnificent effort on
the part of Lieut. Lay and so typically Australian—he didn't
wait to get permission from his Company Commander, but
just acted!

This happened two nights before Christmas Day—an ever
to be remembered Christmas period.

Christmas Day, 1917

It was my custom of an afternoon to visit the Reserve Company and explain the work for that night. On this occasion I found five officers of the company having a little Christmas Day celebration. No extra Christmas rations had been served out to the troops but the batmen had scrounged some tins of bully beef from the Quartermaster's Store and with this as a basis, together with some German sausage and potatoes found in a German dugout and some army biscuits, had made a sort of stew. They also souvenired a jar of rum. The brand of the rum marked on the jar in big letters, S.R.D., was nick-named by the Diggers 'Seldom Reaches Destination'— meaning it never got to the troops in the front line but was collared by the line of communication troops on the way up!

In view of this celebration I spoke only a few words about the night's work, saying, 'I will see you all at Stokes Corner at half past seven tonight.' This I did, splitting the party up into three groups each of about twenty men, spread along the 800 yards of the battalion front on which I was working.

The night was as bright as day—the winter crisp air and the frozen ground reflecting the light of the full moon. Every now and then the unavoidable striking of a pick against an angle iron picket as it was driven into the ground resounded with a loud clang as metal hit metal, the noise ringing loudly in the still night over No Man's Land. It was not long before the Huns heard and saw the working party and opened up with machine gun fire on the party working on our extreme left. No Man's Land was about 400 yards wide at that point and I was on the extreme right of the section that I was working on when this happened.

Keeping inside our line I ran down the 300 yards towards the threatened spot to find the working party had abandoned their job and were collected in a bunch about 200 yards to the rear behind a 'strongpost.' I ordered them back on to the job, made them pick up their tools and start work again but as it was too risky for them to continue working, I then gave the order for them to retire in proper formation. The men, instead of resenting this order to return, quite freely and willingly obeyed it. In their hearts they knew that they had behaved badly but they were under a weak N.C.O. and the company officer in charge of them, having started the work left them to it and retired to the safety of the company headquarters in that part of the line. Some of the men told me afterwards—'we knew we had funked it and were all shivery but your order put new heart into us! We were soldiers!'

This was a typical case of the way that the digger respected command and did so well in the war, completely contrary to the view held by many English officers that Australians were an ill-disciplined lot. Far from that, I never saw an occasion during the whole of the war in which an order given by an officer was not immediately obeyed. The weak officer referred to in this case was reported and transferred out of the battalion.

The following morning when I was at battalion head-quarters giving my report on the night's work to the Acting C.O. (the C.O. being on leave to England), the Brigadier, Brigadier-General Leane strode into our dugout. He had come from the 5th Battalion next in line to us, and was obviously not too pleased with what he saw or was told about the defence work being carried out on their front. He started straight away, 'Good morning. I have come to talk about your works!' 'Well Sir, here is Joynt, the battalion works officer just come in. He can tell you everything,' the Acting C.O. replied. 'I will ask YOU questions,' the Brigadier replied, 'and YOU will give me answers! Now, how far does your wire stretch from (naming a point on the map)?' ————, who had not once been up to see the work himself leaving the whole thing to me replied by pointing to a position on the map. The Brigadier asked, 'have you been working on that line all the week?' 'Yes Sir,' replied ————. 'Well, how is it when I was here last week you had reached this position?' asked the Brigadier pointing to a spot several hundred yards in advance of the position he had just named. Seeing the pickle ———— was in, I butted in trying to help him get clear of the Brigadier's clutches by saying, 'Sir, that is not the position the Brigadier means, that spot was passed days ago. We have started another line which is now up to this spot,' pointing with my fingers on the map to the second line of wire I was running. The Brigadier, seeing he was being bluffed a bit then attacked me by saying, 'my Acting Staff Captain tells me Joynt is not taking his job seriously enough. Yesterday afternoon my Staff Captain heard him giving his instructions to the working party commander in a very offhand and loose manner, without any detail at all.' 'Oh, Sir,' I replied, 'I can account for that. When I arrived at the reserve company headquarters I found them all cele-brating Christmas and ———— (naming an 8th Battalion officer who had been seconded to Headquarters to act as an Acting Staff Captain) broke in and started chipping me with questions concerning the works programme. Shut up Andy,' I said, 'it is Christmas Day—I don't want to disturb the festivities, I will see you all at 7.30.' 'What!' said the Briga-dier, 'you dare to tell me that you told one of my Staff officers to shut up!' and with that he told me off properly and then stormed out of the dugout.

'You made a great mistake,' ———— said to me. 'Never argue with the Brigadier, he will have you "in the gun" and now you will never do any good in the Battalion—I never argue with him.'

That night, whilst I was on the job, two engineer officers turned up from Brigade headquarters. I knew them both and said, 'I suppose you have been sent by the Brigadier to

have a look over the works?' 'Yes,' they replied. After they
had had a good look around I asked for their report. 'Very
good indeed!' they replied. 'Will you give that report to the
Brigadier?' I asked, 'because I believe he has me "in the gun".'
'Not at all,' the senior engineer officer replied, 'it was refresh-
ing to him to have you stand up to him. It is ————— with
whom he is annoyed. Anyhow, we will hand in a good report
so far as it affects the 8th Battalion's defences you have
erected.'

On Boxing Night I asked the company in the line to provide a patrol to go out and reconnoitre No Man's Land to
see how far we could go in safety with a further line of wire
that I had started to run. The corporal in charge of the
patrol came back quickly to tell me, 'if you continue along
the line you are now working on we will just about wire in
a Hun forward listening post.' Of course, I ceased work
immediately on that line and withdrew the working party.

Afterwards, throughout the battalion and brigade I
suffered a lot of good-natured chaffing over the incident. The
story became exaggerated to the extent that I had actually
wired in a Hun post!

Thus ended my own Christmas Festivities for the year
1917.

During the past three months whilst we were building up
our defences No Man's Land became our land because we
obtained such superiority over the Huns in patrolling. Our
patrols, over and over again, drove off Hun patrols and whenever the Huns attempted a raid, they usually ended up by
losing a lot of casualties without gaining any of the prisoners
they wanted badly so as to obtain identification of the divisions facing them in Flanders. On the contrary our raids,
which were frequent for the same reason, were always successful. This applied to the whole of the Anzac front of five
divisions covering about six miles, each division vying with

the other to see who could capture the most German prisoners.

20th March 1918

Tremendous bombardment by both our own and the enemy's guns on our front nearly all the night and day, particularly in the early morning. Our S.O.S. went up at 5.30 calling for a machine gun barrage, later 'intelligence' showed that Fritz had attempted a raid and had been hit back leaving ten men killed on our wire and five prisoners in our hands. The 12th Battalion were responsible for this splendid performance.

21st March 1918

To the surprise of all ranks all fatigues were suspended for the day. The reason for this became obvious when information was received by wire that at 4.30 a.m. intense artillery fire had commenced all along the whole British and French fronts. Followed later in the day by another wire from Army H.Q. to the effect that the Huns had attacked at 8 o'clock in the morning on a 50 mile front on the 3rd and 5th Army fronts (Arras to St. Quentin) and that, except for our outpost line—which had fallen—our battle line was holding.

22nd March 1918

Another wire came through to the effect that the Huns had captured Vaulx-Vauxcourt, a village about 3 or 4 miles behind our front line and that we had driven him out by a counter-attack. The men are all wonderfully confident that Fritz will fail in his great attack and although many rumours are floating around they are nearly all optimistic ones. The great attack has come in the very place where we all knew it was coming. Since yesterday morning the Huns have not fired a shot on our front and the place is weirdly uncanny in its silence—like us, Fritz must be moving his troops and guns down south.

23rd March 1918

Tonight at mess an order was passed round that all fatigue and working parties for tomorrow were cancelled—this made us wonder but later on another order came for all companies to withdraw their wardens who were forward at the 2nd Zone defence line. This second order determined us in deciding that our Division, or at any rate our brigade was going south to help stem the great attack. Mess became very lively in consequence—especially as the health of Major Eller our second-in-command was drunk as he is leaving the battalion tomorrow morning for six months leave to Australia. In his reply he told us that he could not but feel sorry at the thought of leaving us on the eve of such big battles being fought by the battalion. After mess the Colonel was called away to a conference at Brigade H.Q. When he returned he called the company commanders together and told us we were not going down south straight away, but were going to relieve the 54th Battalion of our 5th Division that had received orders to move to the Somme. They were holding the Line where we were once before at Christmas time (Wytschaete), when I was battalion Works Officer.

The Colonel also brought back the news from Brigade that the big Hun attack was being delivered at a density of troops never before dreamt of—no less than three divisions on a 200 yard front and waves of men five miles deep with field guns behind the waves. A total of 80 Hun divisions were attacking on one of our Army fronts. In other words, more troops than are in the British Army altogether were concentrated against only one of our Army sectors. Forty divisions made the attack the first day at about 9 o'clock in the morning, in a deep fog. Our line resisted so stubbornly that at the end of the day's fighting our splendid Tommies had beaten back every attack made upon them—three divisions, notably the 3rd, 51st and 9th had done particularly well, the 51st Scottish division resisting an attack by eight enemy divisions and at the end of the day still held their ground.

24th March 1918

A Battalion Movement order was issued about midday. By that time all companies had held a Marching Out Parade, checked all equipment, ammunition etc., and made up shortages, cleaned up the lines and stood ready to move. I had finished paying the men of my company and after balancing my acquittance rolls found I had only a balance of fr. 1400 to return to the Adjutant. This was a relief to me as the idea of moving into action with the whole of the men's pay in my possession was not too comforting to me. The Movement Order directed us to march out at 6 o'clock in the evening with one blanket rolled—packs and valises to be left at Battalion Store.

Before the company dismissed I read to them the latest Official Bulletin containing the war news of the Great Hun Offensive. I think there was hardly a man in the company who was not disappointed that we were not to march straight away down to the Somme to help in beating back the brutal Hun. I was in charge of the parade, as Capt. Campbell, with all other company commanders, had proceeded with the C.O. to reconnoitre our new position in the line at Messines Ridge.

As the battalion was moving by platoons at 200 yards distance and our company marched last, we did not fall in until 6.30. After a march of about 6 miles we reached our position and took over from a captain of the 54th Battalion, 5th Division. It was one o'clock in the morning before I was able to turn in.

25th March 1918

Our company was ordered to provide a wiring party of three
N.C.O's. and 20 men under an officer. I decided to take this
party myself and start the wiring of a post in the front line
that No. 16 Platoon was down to occupy when it came to
'D' Coy's. turn to take over the front system of defence. We
set off at 7.30 p.m. and carried our wiring stores up to the
job from Preston Dump, the rearward supply dump. We
wired a line of about 120 yards in front of the post. We
suffered no casualties and returned to our lines about 1
o'clock in the morning.

26th March 1918

At 5 o'clock we 'stood to' as is usual for all forward troops,
an hour before daylight. This meant that I had had only 3
hours sleep and only 4 hours the night before.

More war news came through during the day to say that
our troops were being gradually forced back in places but
were now holding positions on the right. Bapaume, Le
Tronsley-High Wood and Peronne were now in the enemy's
hands but the French were rapidly coming to our aid and
had taken over portion of our 5th Army front, they were
now under a French General (Fulotte) and our reinforcing
divisions were arriving well. Also, many French divisions
had been taken from the Flanders front and sent down to the
Somme.

At 9 o'clock our company moved up and relieved 'C' Coy.
who in turn relieved 'A' Coy. in the outpost line, who came
back to our vacated position of No. 2 Reserve Coy. in
Oosterverne Wood.

Lieut. Pitt took charge of the wiring party—during the
evening there suddenly opened a most intense bombardment
of light shells on our Front. We all thought the wiring
parties would be cut to pieces but when they returned they
reported no casualties. Fritz had evidently seen the parties

and got scared that we were going to attack as he sent up numbers of different flares and opened up a rapid machine gun fire, followed by his artillery and trench mortars.

27th March 1918

At 4 o'clock this morning Fritz repeated his performance by suddenly bringing down a most intense barrage on our Front Line posts for about an hour. We suffered no casualties. The weather has unexpectedly turned very cold and the last two days there have been frosts which we feel very much after the warm summer weather that we have been experiencing lately, particularly as we handed in to the Q.M. Store our winter clothing. I shivered all day—trying to get to sleep on my wire netting bunk with nothing underneath and only one blanket on top.

Lieut. McGinn took charge of the night wiring party. After the evening meal I went for a walk around the Reserve Posts and then down to the cookhouse in the rear where the meals are cooked and placed in containers (large cans) which are then strapped on mules and carried up to near the front line from where they are man-handled to the outpost positions. The night passed in absolute quietness. Fritz is too busy, I think, trying to fight his way through to Paris on the Somme to worry much about his line up here.

28th March 1918

We arranged the breakfast this morning so that the men can have it at the end of 'Stand-down'—they can then get to sleep and have nothing to disturb them until lunch. By this means, instead of having breakfast at 8 or 9 o'clock the men can save two hours precious sleep. Tonight we change over again, this time our Coy. shift up nearer the front line and take over the main Support Line from 'C' Coy. who move up and take over the front line.

This morning, taking a senior N.C.O. from each platoon

and the acting Company Sgt. Major I went up and reconnoitred the posts and Company H.Q. As soon as it was dark
enough our company moved up and took over. We had our
first casualties just before the relief took place, an odd shell
falling in one of our Reserve posts wounding two men so
severely that one died soon afterwards (Pte. Wallace).

1st & 2nd April 1918

Our battalion carried out a raid on Whiz Farm at 1.30 a.m.
in the morning which was very successful, except that Lieut.
Davidson, our battalion Intelligence Officer is missing and
one man died of wounds (one of my old corporals of 'B'
Coy.). Lieut. Blackman had charge with Lieuts. Tickle,
Murdock and Davis. They killed about 40 Huns and took
five prisoners. Owing to the raid our company had to do an
extra night in the trenches so as not to have a new company
in the line in case Fritz counter-attacked. During the night
a message was received from H.Q. stating information had
been received by an intercepted wireless message that suggested an attack on our Front that night so our patrols were
doubled and all precautions taken.

I told off Company H.Q'trs. (25 men) into Reserve Posts
round C.H.Q. and issued them with two bombs each and
made every precaution if Fritz should try his hand at attacking us. At 1.30 our guns opened a barrage, preceded by a
Gas Projector attack and our raiders 'hopped out.' Fritz
soon sent his S.O.S. up but his artillery reply was very feeble
and very late.

3rd April 1918

'A' Coy. relieved us in the outposts. The night was fearfully
dark and raining—it was a most miserable night.

4th April 1918

Easter week has passed for us in the trenches. Good Friday,
the 29th March was just as lively as any other day, if any-

thing the Huns shelled a little more than usual. We slept all day. In the afternoon a note came round from B.H.Q. saying that we were going to be relieved the next day by a battalion of the 21st British Division. Soon afterwards an officer of the company that was to take over our Reserve position appeared. His Battalion was the 12/13th Northumberland Fusiliers and they had just come up from the fighting on the Somme, where they had been relieved by our 3rd Division. The C.O., a Major came along later and also got particulars from us as to how we ran things, meals, stand-to's, reliefs etc. He had tea with us and told us our 3rd Division had done splendidly on the Somme. They had put fresh heart into the tired Tommies the way they had marched into action singing and whistling, and they were hardly in position before they 'hopped' over and took 400 prisoners and killed an equal number of Bosches.

I spent the afternoon in handing over to the 2nd in command of the company of the Northumberland Fusiliers who were to relieve my company at 6 o'clock in the evening.

By 6.30 our Relief was complete. 'D' Coy. marched away to our old billets, Doncaster Huts at Locre but I was detailed as Entraining officer to see the forward companies away from the Light railway siding at Warsaw N.24.C9.2. It was 2.30 in the morning before all the troops were clear and I sent the train away. The Relief by the Northumberland Fusiliers was the most unsatisfactory one ever carried out by our Battalion. The Englishmen were terribly new at the game and very frightened, many of them were new men sent over from England, some of them were actually crying when ordered to their places in the outpost line. To add to this, the Forward company had not brought their Lewis guns with them. This meant that the relief had to be held up until the N.F. had sent back 5 miles to get their guns and bring them up. The reports of the hand-over relief that

I got all referred to the difficulty in making the Tommy officers aware of the general situation. They asked few questions, such as how far out does 'No Man's Land' extend; what are the dangerous spots that need watching; where do my flanks extend to; etc. etc. Some of our officers were loath to 'hand over' saying it was a cruel shame that men should be in charge of such uninspiring officers. They arranged to leave their own Lewis guns with the Tommies until their own guns turned up.

This all delayed me getting the 'All Clear' signal to send my report to Battalion Headquarters 'Relief OK.' It was nearly 5 o'clock in the morning by the time I turned in after travelling from Warsaw to La Clyte by light railway and then marching to Locre.

5th April 1918

At 7 o'clock we were astir and our valises were rolled up (we had slept in them for only two hours, the first time for 9 days). We 'fell in' at 8 o'clock and marched to the 'embussing point' where we were told off into motor waggons and began our trip to Strazelle (4 hours run). Here we went into billets but not for long as 'D' Coy. was ordered out at 4 o'clock and marched away to the railway station where the 5th Battalion and our company entrained for the Somme. At 8.15 p.m. our train steamed out—the men were in trucks (35 to each) and the officers had carriages. There were five of us in one compartment so we were all able to lie down and have a good sleep all night, not awaking till 8 o'clock next morning when we reached our destination, Hangast, midway between Abbeville and Amiens.

6th April 1918

Here we detrained and marched away to a quiet spot along the road where we rested for an hour, had a wash in the

Somme River, a brush up and breakfast. Continuing our march we reached our billeting area at St. Ouen, a march of about 7 kilos or 4 miles, about 1 o'clock. The French villagers were very dejected over the war and very scared that the Huns were going to capture Amiens their beautiful city about 10 miles away. Our billets were splendid ones and Madam could not do enough for us, making us clean beds and preparing coffee for us immediately on our arrival. I turned in right away as I was not feeling well and slept all the afternoon. At 5 o'clock the remainder of the battalion marched in headed by the Pipe Band. The local citizens were overjoyed at seeing the Australians and made us little presents—saying 'English no bon, Australien tres bon.' 'No vin pour Anglais.' 'Beaucoup vin pour Australiens.' These poor people looked upon us as their rescuers and cheered up considerably when we appeared on the scene. This is our third appearance on the Somme and on each of the two previous occasions the Australians have made a name for themselves.

Terrible stories were told by the French people of the disgraceful behaviour of the English troops during the retreat —for such it appears to be. The newspapers make out that it was a withdrawal, but panic and a disgusting stampede appears to be nearer the mark. English no bon was heard everywhere we went.

The doctor found two French women crying their eyes out over the fate of their beloved France and the threatened destruction of their beautiful city of Amiens, which was now being shelled and knocked to pieces by German bombs. Being only 10 miles away from the city the Huns, having made the big advance of 35 miles to the south of Amiens, would have advanced to the north of Amiens as well had it not been for the entrance of the 3rd and 4th Australian Divisions which were sent down from Flanders to help stem the tide.

8th April 1918

The Commanding Officer held a conference of officers commanding companies and those officers who were going to command companies when we went into action. He told us what he knew about the tactical situation and what we were to do—viz. to relieve the 3rd Australian Division at Ribemont, near Bresle: the 1st and 3rd Brigades in the line and the 2nd in support. We were to be prepared to move at a moment's notice, even while he spoke a 'runner' brought a message from Bde H.Q. ordering us to move to Vignicourt at once, so we rushed off and soon had our companies fallen in and the battalion marched away. The old Mayor was almost in tears and took comfort from my assurance that the Bosches would not get as far as his beloved town—the Australians would see to that. 'Australien Soldat tres bon', he said. Women, children and all turned out to see us away. Just as we moved Capt. Campbell was recalled to act as Town Major and I took over the command of the company. We reached Vignicourt about 6 o'clock—it was only about 7 kilos march—and I soon got the men billeted. The town was in a state of semi-desertion, some people still stayed behind especially the Estaminet people who were selling French beer and wine to the troops at even a faster rate than usual as we had paid the men as soon as we reached town. There was no accommodation for officers so we spread out all over the town looking for a suitable place to spend the night. At last we made arrangements with a very excitable French woman, who kept an Estaminet, to have an upper room in her house which she consented to as soon as we procured 'Le papier' from the Mayor.

9th April 1918

The following day we were moving again by 9 o'clock for Querrieu which was about 6 miles behind the line—we had a 9 kilo march so we halted at midday for lunch and the 'cookers' which were following had tea ready for the troops. We halted an hour, then the bugles blew the 'fall in' and off we went again. Soon afterwards we entered the town of Querrieu. The Pipe Band heading the column swung round at the square and halting played each company into the town, the C.O. standing in front and looking critically at his men marching in. As company commander I rode at the head of my company and felt pride when we swung into the main street and marched through with all the available 'Line of Communication' troops in the town lining the roadway to watch us march past. We came as saviours.

10th April 1918

How different this town looked now from what it was last May when my brother and I passed through it on our way to spend the weekend in Amiens—it was then an Army Corps Headquarters, now it was a Brigade Headquarters and the little Estaminet where we had drunk some French beer was wrecked and looted. It turned all our Australian hearts sick to see the looting that had gone on by the Tommy troops. Houses had been ransacked, drawers and cupboards had been pulled out and the contents emptied on the floor in their search for plunder. No wonder the French people hated them and I believed now the stories of the French people that soldiers had jostled the refugees out of the way in their hurry to get away from the Hun. The house where we were billeted had been the house of a well-to-do merchant, a textile manufacturer and his factory adjoined his premises. All the rooms were just as the men and girls had jumped up and left them when they fled for their lives. The pity of it all filled our stout fellows' hearts with anger and I think if they had seen any Tommies about they would have shot them.

The cellars had been drunk dry and bottles were strewn around in hundreds. The C.O. issued a special 'Order of the Day' to the effect that, 'For the Honour of Australia, and so as not to be coupled with the English "Harrier Battalions" men should abstain from looting or damaging the property of our French allies.'

12th April 1918

At about 11 o'clock in the morning, just as we were about to move to relieve a battalion of the 3rd Division, an order came for all company commanders to report to the C.O. immediately. When I attended the C.O. flung me a new map with Hazebrouck on it and said—'There is your new map Joynt. The Huns have broken through up north and they are sending us back again. We are to hold ourselves in readiness to move at any moment and when we reach our destination be prepared to get out of the train and go straight into the fight.' All valises, packs and everything we possessed except our fighting kit were to be dumped and left behind and we were not even to take a blanket. Overcoats were allowed (which turned out very lucky for us before the finish).

We stood by waiting for our marching orders for the rest of that day. It appears there was some trouble with the French railways, Amiens railway station was heavily shelled and the station staff had cleared out. At 10 o'clock that night we moved out. Captain Campbell returned from his job as Area Commandant and again took charge of the Company. We marched away with pipe band playing and drums beating for our 8 or 9 miles march to Amiens. We were scheduled to entrain from Le Roche station at 3.42 a.m. but on nearing Amiens the column was held up for two hours as the Huns were again shelling the station and the station civilian staff had again cleared out.

We marched through Amiens at 4 o'clock in the morning, the whole city was deserted and deathly quiet. The battalion bivouacked for breakfast in the Boulevard. The civilian railway staff having returned to the station we went aboard our train at about 8 o'clock in the morning, nearly four hours behind schedule. Companies 'B', 'C' and 'D' and Details were on the one train, 'A' company was to follow by a later train. We travelled all day and towards evening it was quite apparent that we were nearing the Battle Zone. Crowds of refugees could be seen streaming away from the front areas carting all they could of their worldly possessions with them. Villages were burning in the distance and ambulances full of wounded were making their way to the rear Casualty Clearing Stations.

We reached a siding and commenced detraining when one of our Divisional Staff Officers drove up and ordered us in the train again. The Huns were advancing on Hazebrouck, they had broken the English Divisions out in front and had no one to stop them. We were to push on in the train to Hazebrouck siding, detrain and go straight out and take up a position in front of Nieppe Forest to defend Hazebrouck. The 1st Brigade which was following us was to be on the left when it arrived and the 2nd in the centre, the 3rd on our right. Our Division was to cover a front of about six to ten miles, the distance usually held by five divisions. The four British divisions who held that front were out in the blue completely disorganized—lost—nobody appeared to know where they were or even where the Huns were. They were the 31st Division (which included the Guards Brigade and South Africans, the 29th, the 40th and the 50th). Nobody knew whether they were still fighting or if they had all been captured. Our 7th Battalion had moved up earlier and thrown out a screen to cover our Brigade while we dug in. Hun patrols had been seen to the south, well around our flank, so went the report.

When the train reached Hazebrouck about dusk we hurriedly detrained. All our packs and blankets had been stacked and rolled in bundles and trucked with us so as each man marched off the station he was made to take a pack and every tenth man carried a roll of blankets. These were all carried out and dumped where the Brigade waggon lines were to be established about a thousand yards from the railway station to be safer from possible enemy shelling of the railway station area. We were not to see our packs again for seven days. Some good person had arranged for hot cocoa to be ready and every man got a pannikin full—this was to be our only meal for the next twenty-four hours, as we had no iron rations with us.

We 'piled arms' by companies in selected areas over a wide front and laid down between the ranks to rest. But soon instructions came for all Company Commanders to report to Battalion Headquarters. It was already dark and I had to pick my way to an adjoining farmhouse where Battalion Headquarters had been temporarily set up. I found the other Company Commanders already there in an inside room. Blankets covered all the windows and the C.O., Adjutant and other Company Commanders were poring over a map with the aid of a single candle stuck in a bottle. The C.O's. demeanour was serious and calm, but the atmosphere was dramatic and tense as he informed us of the position, read the latest intelligence report from Division and unfolded and gave details of the role of the 1st Australian Division and in particular, the orders and details for the 8th Battalion's advance to its allotted defensive position about seven miles away. He pointed out that our efforts for the next few days were in the nature of a forlorn hope and explained how the enemy, after draining off most of the British Divisions from the Belgian Front to go to the assistance of General Gough's army down on the Somme, had assembled another huge army and suddenly opened a major offensive in the northern sector of the British Army front designed to break through and capture the great British bases of Calais, Boulogne and Le Havre, the main supply bases on the

Channel coast. The enemy had struck suddenly and unexpectedly and had completely overrun the four British Divisions defending that sector.

Outnumbered and already battle weary from their work on the Somme as part of the 3rd Army, from whence they had been relieved, they were believed to be still fighting a rear guard action out in front but all organization had broken down and nobody knew exactly where they were. The role of the 1st Australian Division was to fill the breach, stop the rot and hold a line until the Channel Ports could be evacuated or until reinforcements could be brought up and a new line of defence organized. We were to understand that there was no other formed body of troops capable or able to put up a fight between us and the Channel Ports. Our 7th Battalion who had arrived on a previous train had already moved out and were providing a screen on a very wide front for the deployment of the 8th Battalion, which in turn was to move at once and try to reach the far side of Nieppe Forest a distance of about seven miles away and then divide the front and extend the line to the left so as to cover the two main enemy approach roads leading through the village of Vieux Berquin. The 5th and 6th Battalions were following and would arrive by later trains and go into support. The dispositions of the 8th Battalion were 'C' Company on the right, 'B' Company in the centre and 'D' Company on the left. 'A' Company (two platoons only—the other two platoons were coming up on another train) were to act as Battalion Reserve and support until the arrival of the 6th Battalion, so spoke the Colonel and then turning to me said, 'Joynt, you move first and try to reach this point,' pointing on the map to a farm house that commanded the exit of any enemy troops deploying from the cover of the village, 'and take up a defensive line from that point covering a front of about a mile to where another main road enters our front. You will be responsible for the defence of that road until tomorrow morning, when the 1st Battalion 1st Brigade should arrive and go into position to extend your left. Until then you have an open left flank. My Head-quarters will be here (pointing to another dot on the map about a thousand yards in the rear) so run a flanking patrol during the night to protect my Headquarters from that direction. Now move at once! Take adequate precautions as you move through the main road through the forest as you do not know when you may run into the Hun's advancing patrols, or even their main forces. Absolute silence must be observed. When you are in position report to me by runner.'

I hastened back to where I had left my Company to find them all sleeping or resting between the lines of 'Piled Rifles.'

Without having the men disturbed because every bit of rest they got at this time was important, I got hold of my four Platoon Commanders and my 2 I/C and explained first the tactical situation, allotted to them their inter-platoon boundaries and then where my Company Headquarters would be established IF we were successful in reaching our allotted line. My Platoon Commanders were all top-class officers, very experienced, sound and the sort that needed no spurring on. They each had their particular characteristics and I posted them to their areas accordingly. My left open flank I gave to Pitt, a young Englishman who had emigrated to Australia just before the war broke out and like thousands of others, had joined the A.I.F. immediately on the outbreak of war. He was very steady, not the kind to be stampeded just because the enemy had got round his flank. 2/Lieut. Bourke, quietly spoken although of Irish temperament had been recently promoted from the ranks—I posted him next from the left and gave him about 400 yards of ground to cover which was, going by the map, all open fallowed country giving an excellent field of fire and covering the approaches to both Pitt's post and my centre post under McGinn, whose post was to be slightly advanced in order to take advantage of the cover provided by a small copse. McGinn, a young man promoted from a sergeant, was an Anzac with plenty of dash whom I knew would not miss any opportunity of exploiting a situation or taking advantage of any ground features that would give an added field of fire or of moving forward temporarily in order to engage an enemy target to advantage. On my right, in front of my Company Headquarters on the road leading direct from the village of Vieux Berquin and connecting up with 'B' Company's left post I placed Lieutenant Fenton. A bit elderly for a lieutenant he was a school teacher, calm, solid and as steady as they make them—in short, absolutely reliable.

Having hurriedly gone over the plan of defence as outlined with them and being satisfied that each Platoon Commander thoroughly understood his job and the 2 I/C (Lieut. K. Stevenson) had what little information I had to give him about rations, etc. I then got the Company S/M to call the Company up and I addressed them briefly. I told them what I knew and gave them the picture, reminding them that perhaps never before had an occasion arisen where so much depended on the action of each individual man during the next twenty-four hours. If our one hundred and twelve rifles could hold up the enemy on our particular mile of front, which was the main approach route to the town of Hazebrouck (an important railway junction in the defence of Calais), it would be possible for us to still win the war. I told them that in consequence, once we marched out from here there would be no coming back and that in fact we were going out to dig our graves. This talk instead of depressing them had the effect I knew it would.

Never have I been so proud of Australians as I was that night. They were irrepressible. As we marched by platoons, at 200 yards interval along that dark road leading through the dense forest of Nieppe, knowing not the moment when we would be stopped by enemy fire the men cracked jokes and from time to time I had to send messages along the column to 'stop that whistling' and 'be quiet.' For a time only the sound of an occasional rattle of a piece of equipment would be heard and then the sound of 'Tipperary' or 'Colonel Bogey' and other marching songs would be heard again—it was impossible to suppress their high spirits. Again and again the C.O. sent messages to me, 'to stop my men making such a noise' but the men had their tails right up— they had the honour and reputation of Australia in their hands—and every man seemed to have imbibed the thrill of the situation. They were 'going to show them'—i.e. the Tommies. I really believe it was the greatest moment of their lives. They needed not the inspiration of Lord Haig's famous 'Order of the Day', copies of which had been issued to Company Commanders just before we moved off but which I had not bothered to read to the men—I did not think it necessary. This message to the troops of the British Army, after describing the threat of this second great Hun offensive, stated inter alia—'Nothing now remains, but believing in the justice of our cause. With our backs to the wall, to fight it out to the last man!'

We had been told when we detrained to wait for rations but eventually had to go without any, but we were able to get our Regimental Reserve of tools to take in—fifteen shovels and several picks. It was about one o'clock in the morning when we moved off, scouts out in front and 'D' Company leading, followed by 'C' and 'B' Companies. The Colonel and Adjutant preceded the column for the first mile. We passed along deserted villages and farm houses all the inhabitants having fled that afternoon. From time to time by the aid of an electric torch the C.O. and Adjutant examined the map—we were working entirely by map and compass. Because of the uncertainty of things we were very careful to cover up the light of the torch in case any Hun patrols might be in the vicinity. After much discussion at various crossroads and turnings we at last arrived at the spot where my Company was to dig in. As I had told my Platoon Commanders their positions before we moved off all that was necessary for me to do now was to take a bearing with my compass to give them the general line and away they went with their platoons.

From the map I chose for my Company Headquarters a farm on the roadway leading from the village of Vieux Berquin through the Forest of Nieppe that we were to defend. Leaving Lieutenants Fenton and McGinn to pick their own positions I went forward with Lieutenant Bourke to see his platoon placed and then on to Lieutenant Pitt whom I had placed on my extreme left. After seeing these two platoons commence digging I returned and inspected the posts of my two right platoons. Day was just breaking and I found these two platoons had gone forward about 200 yards from the general line to take advantage of a copse and some farm buildings that jutted out from our general line. This formed a dangerous salient in our line but I thought the farm houses and copse should be held by us so I agreed to their dispositions. Unfortunately this was an error of judgment as it allowed Fenton's post to be enfiladed from a three-storey Mill about 300 yards on his right. Later, however, when the C.O. did his rounds he approved these positions.

By this time the sound of fighting was quite audible, the sound of machine guns could be heard in the distance and shells were beginning to fall in our vicinity. On returning to the farm where my Company Headquarters had already established themselves I found them very comfortably installed in a big farm house with many outbuildings and barns. The farm had evidently been owned by a well-to-do farmer and the furnishings and beds were of the best. The house contained over a dozen rooms with accommodation if necessary, including the barns, for several hundred men to sleep.

The bombed and deserted St Roche Railway Station at Amiens, where the 7th Battalion suffered casualties whilst loading their transport. *Source:* A.W.M.

A post of the 7th Battalion at the western edge of Nieppe Forest, 18 April 1917. While Front Line posts were usually in trenches, some, like this one, were built up breastworks because of excessive water on the flats. *Source:* A.W.M.

D Coy, 8th Battalion, headquarters—the farmhouse and huge barn where hundreds of retreating Tommies were given shelter and rest. *Source:* A.W.M.

The gramophone and one of the five French quadrille records which were found in the farmhouse which became D Coy's H.Q.

Men of the 6th and 8th Battalions in old trenches north of the railway—
the scene of the brave initiatives by Capt. A. Campbell, O.C., and D. Coy.
Source: A.W.M.

Men of the 46th Battalion in the Hindenburg Outpost Line. The wire
entanglement through which they had attacked can be seen at the back of
the trench. *Source:* A.W.M.

A Commander worthy to rank among the greatest war leaders of history—
General Sir John Monash, seated, with some of his senior generals. *Source:*
A.W.M.

Cows, pigs and poultry were in abundance and the boys had just finished milking all the cows they could bail up and as the troops had not had a meal for over twenty-four hours they were busy cooking eggs and plucking fowls and peeling potatoes in preparation for a much needed meal.

Hearing the C.O. had called and gone round to look at my dispositions I hurried along the line to catch up to him. When I did so he was just replacing my left post which he thought too exposed. He approved of all the other posts. To our immediate front was the village of Vieux Berquin with large buildings and a church tower that looked down on and dominated our entire front.

With my runner I went out to the village to have a look back at my defence line—all my posts had a good field of fire and I was satisfied that we would take some shifting. I walked along the main street of this village where it joined my left flank making that position a very hard place to defend, so I was glad the C.O. had withdrawn my line here about 200 yards.

The Huns were already shelling the village and it was pitiful to see French refugees coming slowly along the road— old men and women who had evidently been left in the first mad rush were now helping themselves along with the aid of sticks while German shells fell around them. Some of these people might have been German spies dressed as old women, but I had no time to examine them. As I stood on the side of the road and watched a small party of the Guards Brigade, about twenty men with three officers in the lead marched by. Although some of the men were not 'in step' they were all under control but they looked pretty 'done' and war weary. I never imagined the day would come when I would see the Guards marching out of step, but it was evident they were a remnant. I said 'Good day' to the leader but he never answered me so I let them go. They passed through my lines, no doubt to reform in rear because I heard afterwards that remnants of the Guards Brigade joined in with our 1st Brigade on my left, and helped in the defence of that sector.

I sent a patrol forward from Lieut. Fenton's post to keep in touch with the British and enemy forces and this patrol reported from time to time how things were going, this information I sent on to Battalion Headquarters. Cpl. Whitton took charge of this patrol work and did a very good job until he was killed by the advancing Germans.

Postscript: a 7th Battalion Account

Proceeding along my line to the right I came across an officer of our sister battalion, the 7th—Lieut. Reynolds. He was moving his platoon to join up with the right of the 8th Battalion on a corner of the Nieppe Forest—a dangerous tactical point, he said. He had an interesting story to tell me of how, after detraining at Hazebrouck, they marched out a few miles toward Vieux Berquin and, halting, fell out on the side of the road for a ten-minute halt to enable the men to eat their iron rations, consisting of bully beef and biscuits, whilst their company commander rode forward to choose the line of defence. Whilst they were eating, a battery of Tommy artillery galloped past them on the road, shouting out the now familiar cry from the Tommies, 'The Jerries are coming in thousands'. One of his Diggers shouted back, 'Mind you don't get drowned in the Channel'.

He also told me that when his platoon reached Vieux Berquin just as it was getting dark he went forward with a patrol to see if he could get in touch with any troops still fighting. While feeling their way in the dark through a wood, they suddenly heard, about ten yards ahead of them, the challenge 'Halt, who goes there?', delivered in a voice audible for miles. It was a Guardsman, challenging as if he were standing in front of his sentry box at Buckingham Palace. Reynolds assured him that they were not Germans, and the sentry then directed them to his Battalion Headquarters where Reynolds had a chat with their C.O., telling him their intentions. The Colonel said they could hold their line, but asked Reynolds to bring his men and stay with them as their flank troops always fell back and they had to do likewise.

Reynolds also said with wry amusement that when he returned to his own line he found a British major gathering in Tommy stragglers and occupying a beautiful trench with a perfect field of fire, but the Major said that as soon as the Germans appeared en masse, they would all skedaddle. He implored Reynolds to stay with him.

Capt. Bowtell-Harris, O.C. of the 7th's 'C' Company, asked Reynolds to take his platoon and occupy a vital corner of the forest adjoining the right of the 8th Battalion when they came up. A little later they saw a sight that thrilled them—a line of Guards moving towards them at the double with their rifles at the trail, as if on the parade ground. He told them to act as supports and take up a position about 200 yards in their rear, but Capt. Bowtell-Harris, on his right, asked some of them to stay with him. This they were most reluctant to do but he forced them to do so.

Diary continues

When I returned to my Company Headquarters I saw a sight that intrigued me. Was my eyesight playing me tricks? Out on the lawn in front of my farmhouse there were men and women dancing: a gramophone was playing and men and women were dancing to the tune of a French Quadrille —men in frock coats and some in top hats, and women in long dresses and Parisian gowns. What had happened? Had the Belgian occupants of the farm and nearby village gone off their heads in the face of such impending danger? But as I drew near I recognized they were some of the men of my Company Headquarters staff, about 15 of them. What had happened was they had raided Madam's wardrobes and Monsieur's dressing room and donned themselves out in their finery. I could not help bursting with laughter. The absurdity of it all—here, with the Huns almost in shooting range were my Company staff—signallers, stretcher bearers, company clerk, runners and batmen, etc. burlesquing in high spirits when at any moment they would be fighting desperately for their lives against tremendous odds, as our weak company of only 120 men were facing an anticipated attack by at least a German Division (about 12,000 men).

Shouting that the Huns were coming and were almost in sight I gave the order 'Stand To.' My Lewis gun section, some still in women's dress, manned their allotted post, scrambling up through the rafters under the roof of the barn and pointing the barrel of their Lewis gun through a hole made by removing some of the roof tiles. They were soon blazing away as the Huns emerged from the village opposite. I said to my batman, 'take the gramophone into the kitchen Newman, and when the Huns attack us your job will be putting on those French Quadrille records. We may as well have some music to keep our "pecker" up' and this actually happened.

It was now about eleven o'clock in the morning and the long period I had gone without food and sleep made me feel in need of rest but it was no time for 'spelling' as already my Platoon Commanders were sending in messages to the effect that stragglers from the 31st, 29th, 40th and 50th Divisions were drifting back. They were collected and put in our forward posts and under my officers and N.C.O's. When the Huns attacked they did splendidly; but their own officers did not appear—where they were I don't know!

My batman had laid breakfast for me on the main dining room table—boiled chicken and potatoes. I was thrilled at it all, so different from trench warfare where we usually eat our rations squatting down in 'funk holes.'

At about four o'clock in the afternoon I received word from Lieut. Pitt on No. 4 post that the 29th Division were falling back over his sector thoroughly demoralized and that he found it impossible to rally them, so I hurried along to see what was doing. As I had used up all my runners during the day's work I took a fellow of the Kings Own Yorkshire Light Infantry—a chap whom my piquet on the road had earlier stopped from running and had sent in to Company H.Q. to be kept under surveillance—I ordered him to come with me and he did so reluctantly. I told him all he had to do was to follow about 15 yards behind me and if I got shot take my papers off me and make his way back to Company H.Q. and report it and off we started.

We reached the far end of my lines without mishap and after I had sized up the situation there I turned to the Tommy and said, 'now we will get back, just do what you were doing before.' The Tommy jumped forward saying, 'I am all right Sir, I am all right. I will go anywhere with you but I have never seen officers act like this and have never had decent officers in charge of me before.' The story went the rounds and became the joke of the Company afterwards, but like most stories, retold it became exaggerated—how I made this run-away man into a soldier and in doing so, frightened about nine lives out of him.

On the way back I found the plain in front of my centre posts alive with Tommies, some digging in, others falling back. A Major of the 31st Division was there trying to organize them, a very gallant chap too, but he would insist on keeping the Tommies out in front of my men because, as he said, he had been informed that 'the Australians were their supports' and so they (the Tommies) would take up a line in front of us. He would not listen to reason so I had to let them dig on knowing by the look of them that when the Huns did attack they would all run and leave the place to us.

What English officers were there were useless. I did attempt to get some to work but gave it up. I 'collared' two English Lieutenants and gave them each a sector telling them 'take charge here, collect all the men you can and fill a gap that due to the length of front I had to cover existed between two of my own posts.' They started to do this but as soon as I left the sector to continue on my 'rounds' they both cleared out. I saw them go running towards the forest and told my batman, 'go and get someone with you to follow those officers and when you catch them up, ask them for their names and Regiments. They probably won't tell you so threaten to shoot them if they won't tell you. Report back to me what happens.' After an hour they returned saying they couldn't catch the officers up, they chased them for a mile or two but they ran too fast.

Lieutenant McGinn sent me word that he had the Colonel, Adjutant and Intelligence Officer of the 1st Lancashire Fusiliers, 29th Division, in his post and as soon as I could I went out to see them. When I got to the post I found the Intelligence Officer there but the Colonel and his Adjutant had gone off into the village opposite. McGinn told me that when the Colonel stumbled into his post he greeted McGinn with these words—'Boy, is this your Post?' 'Yes Sir,' replied McGinn. 'You are going to make a fight of it?' 'Yes Sir.' 'Well, give me a rifle, I am one of your men,' and seizing a rifle offered to him he jumped into the Post. The Colonel said his battalion had been fighting a rearguard action for over three days. McGinn then told me that this Colonel was so disgusted with his officers and men who had retreated from their previous positions without orders, this being the first time in the long history of the Regiment that such a thing had occurred that he could not contain himself. He kept muttering away and apologizing for the behaviour of his Regiment and then, suddenly jumping up said, 'My Boy you can report that the 1st Lancashire Fusiliers held the village to the last man.' He had then gone out with just his Adjutant and a few runners and disappeared into the village opposite. McGinn's men cheered him as with walking stick in his hand he strode out toward the enemy. He had vindicated the honour of his Regiment.

We heard later that when he got to the village he found it unoccupied so sent his Intelligence Officer back to collect some of their own men to counter-attack and hold the village. The Intelligence Officer a really good type and up to the standard of the British officer of tradition, on approaching the village with these men was unable to get near it owing to heavy machine gun fire so it was assumed that the Colonel and his Adjutant were lost, either prisoners or dead, but all night long fighting could be heard going on to the left of the village. Afterwards we learnt that the Colonel had rounded up a lot of men himself and led a counter-attack on the village from the left of our position where the village street entered our lines and some buildings and houses ran close to my No. 4 post giving cover for an approach to and from the village. This act on the part of the English Colonel thrilled my men and did a lot to counter the bad showing of other English officers.

As I neared my Headquarters on the way back an English Major on horseback was galloping up and down shouting to the retreating Tommies 'stop and dig in'—a most gallant chap. I went over to him and told him to let the Tommies retire behind my line of posts on the edge of the forest but like the other English Major he would insist on making the Tommies dig in where they were. He also insisted that the Australians were in support and had not yet come up. I said, 'Not so, look towards the edge of the forest, can't you see my posts there.' 'No I can't,' he said. 'Well, that's a good thing,' I replied, 'if you cannot see them it shows how well they have camouflaged their positions for neither will the Huns see them.' However he was adamant, insisting 'you Australians are only in support'—he pulled out a map and pointed to a line on it where he said his orders were to retire to and there dig in 'and this is it,' he maintained as he held the folded map up for me to see. The wind blew it open and it spread out making a splendid target for the enemy to see which they immediately did. Our conversation ended abruptly, for a light German field gun opened fire on both of us. The first shot whizzed by missing us but hitting a poor calf peacefully feeding about 20 yards from us. 'You can stay,' I said, 'but I am off.' I was about 200 yards out in front of the line of my posts, I quickly ran to cover and away the Major galloped. He hadn't gone far when his horse was hit but he continued on foot still shouting 'stop and dig in.' Some of the Tommies did but others we gathered in and put them to strengthen our own posts where they spent the whole day and night in our trenches. It was strange, but there were no junior English officers about to help the Major. Whether they had all been killed or had run away, I know not. The Tommies behaved splendidly when they were mixed up with our fellows and with their help we were able to beat off several German attacks during that night and next day.

When I returned to my Headquarters I found numbers of English Colonels and senior officers who had lost their regiments, but no junior officers. My farmhouse was also full of troops of many regiments who had been gathered up —about 400 altogether—they had been put in the barns by my Company Sgt. Major to lie down and rest amongst the hay. If the Hun had dropped a shell amongst us he would have got a splendid haul.

Private Hocking, a Company signaller, removed some tiles

from the roof and we climbed up on the ceiling of the house which made a splendid observation post. I could see right into the village square opposite where hundreds of Huns were de-bussing and forming up into attack formation. 'We will soon be for it,' I said as we clambered down. Private Hocking wanted to stay and continue observing but I wouldn't let him because when the battle started the roof of the house would be a certain target and would draw an avalanche of shells and machine gun fire and would soon be blown to bits.

My Second-in-Command, Lieut. Keith Stevenson, informed me that an ammunition dump had been discovered about half a mile up the road towards Hazebrouck, but he had no men to go and get some badly needed hand grenades, also rifle grenades, which we would need if it came to 'hand to hand' fighting; so I went down to the cellar where the Signal Section were setting up a signal station with equipment they had brought with them and told Hocking to take another man and find their way to the ammunition dump and get two boxes each of rifle and hand grenades. Be quick about it I said, time is short. The two men jumped to it at once, Signaller Hocking leading the way. Even as I spoke German artillery started shelling the roadway. I had given them a perilous job to do but these two men never hesitated to carry out what was virtually an order—it was broad daylight and their movement down the road presumably could easily be seen from the Hun observation post on the Church steeple in the village. When they did not return after an hour had passed I feared the worst, they must have become casualties. Two hours later Corporal Stewart, the N.C.O. in charge of the Signal Section, reported to me that Hocking had returned with two boxes of bombs but the other chap had been wounded and left at the R.A.P. Hocking's delay was caused because he had helped in taking the place of a stretcher bearer who had been killed when a shell burst right on top of a stretcher bearing party as they were coming down the road. Some other badly wounded men needing help were also assisted by Hocking to get to the R.A.P.

Stewart commended the good work done by Hocking.

The remainder of the day provided plenty of opportunities in the way of shooting because the Hun was so cheeky he persisted in showing himself quite openly, no doubt believing that all resistance had broken down and in consequence our Lewis guns as well as our riflemen got a harvest. Some of the targets engaged were a whole company of Huns at 600 yards range marching in column of fours along the main Vieux Berquin Road. Huns in busses debussing at the Church opposite, only 800 yards away. Other Hun patrols unsuspectingly kept marching up towards our lines to within 40 or 50 yards of our posts before we opened fire.

Postscript: Nieppe Forest

The following is Bean's account of some of these events.

With 1,000 yards to defend with about 120 bayonets, Joynt called his platoon commanders together and told them off to jobs—Pitt, Bourke, McGinn and Fenton, in that order from left to right. Fenton, the senior, was to cover—but not to hold—a big three-storied mill. [later known as the 'Factory'] on the right, beside the Rue du Bois, the road leading from Vieux Berquin to, and along, the northern edge of the forest. Joynt saw from his map that there would be trouble there and was anxious about it.

It was then 1 a.m. on April 13th. The battalion had waited two hours for its transport, and had to start without it, but obtained its reserve of tools—15 shovels and several picks to each company. It moved with the scouts out in front, but had to advance so quickly that the companies didn't attempt to leave the road. Joynt divided one platoon into sections, and then stood at the starting point

with the platoon commander and sent off two men; then
another two just before the others became visible in the
dark; then two more just in sight of them, and so on. He
sent off two sections (14 men) thus: then two sections
in file: then, fifty yards behind them, a platoon in file,
with connecting files between, and then the two remaining
platoons fifty yards behind each other with connecting
files. Each platoon was to keep the men ahead in sight.
This gave, in all, protection to about 200 yards' depth.

THE MIDNIGHT ADVANCE THROUGH NIEPPE FOREST
BY THE 8TH BATTALION, A.I.F.

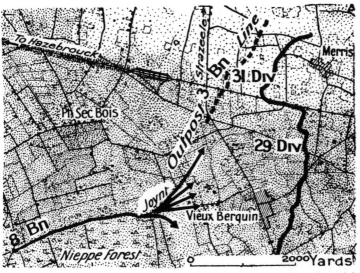

Source: Australian War Memorial

There was no time for more precaution. The first two
men would hear a noise and stop. The others in view of
them would stop. The leading men would either presently
move on of their own accord, or Joynt—who was in his
element, going up and down the line—would send them
on.

They went through empty villages, past empty houses.
They were to go along in strict silence, but their spirits

were up. Joynt told the men, before they moved forward, what the job was. The men were as proud as punch. The Australian units in the south had demonstrated immediately before this what they could do, and the 1st Division was quite sure it could do equally well. Moreover up to then the Australian units had always been on the offensive, but now the time had arrived when (as they had been told by Joynt) we were to 'pick our own line of defence and wait for the Fritzes'; and they said, 'By Cripes, this will do us.' They had also wonderful confidence in their leaders—they knew the best pozzy would be taken up. 'We knew, too,' says Joynt, 'that the situation was critical—we had the notion, "By Cripes, we are going to be licked!" that there was nothing between us and the Channel Ports; and we felt "It's on us!" '*

Diary continues

Hearing that the enemy were employing Armoured Cars I decided to block the road leading from the village into our lines. I placed 20 Tommies at the disposal of my company Sergeant Major who, that night when it was sufficiently dark, dragged out a big French four-wheeled farm waggon and a dray and turned them upside down about 50 yards up the road in front of a post I had established there. These Tommies were then used as a patrol to maintain lateral connection between my two right posts and did splendid work throughout the night.

My posts were so far apart that effective defence of our position depended on stubbornly defending each post by day and active patrolling between the posts at night.

The next day orders came to me recalling men of the 40th Division so I sent a runner round the posts to call in all the men of this Division and then all the men of the other Divisions were gradually recalled until all that was left to me was the 29th Division men.

---

* C.E W. Bean, *Official History of Australia in the War of 1914-18:* The A.I.F. in France 1918 (Sydney 1937), vol. v, pp. 456-7.

15th April 1918

When daylight came the Huns commenced shelling the neighbourhood of my H.Q. and as I had about 80 men of the 29th Division as well as about 25 of my own in the buildings attached to the farm, I ordered the 29th Division men under their only officer (the Divisional Intelligence Officer) to clear out and get under cover behind the hedges in rear and dig themselves in—one very good Sergeant Major of the Lancashire Fusiliers superintended this movement which was done by sending the Tommies three at a time at 50 yards interval, so as not to be observed by the Huns who were looking down from the Vieux Berquin Church tower on to our positions. They had hardly gone when word came to me from my forward post that the Huns were massing in front so I ordered the Tommies to stand by ready in case they were wanted then rang up for the artillery and described the place where the Huns were. Our Artillery soon opened and word came back immediately to the effect that the fire was doing splendid work, shells bursting right over the Huns who had scattered. Things having quietened down a bit I sent the boys of the 29th off to the rear. They were not sorry to go after all they had been through. Their officer was very apologetic over the conduct of his Division and alluded to Gallipoli and how well it had done there fighting with the Australians. Certainly the old 29th had sadly changed and dropped miles in the esteem of our own men but our chaps made allowances for their retreat as they had had a pretty rough time of it.

These men had hardly gone when a man came running in to say that the Huns were attacking my right advanced post (Lieut. Fenton) and he thought the post was nearly blown out by shell fire and trench mortars. I immediately sent him to warn the Company on my right (Captain Fox's Coy.). Almost immediately afterwards Corporal Rainbow came running in from the post to say that the post was wiped out, all the garrison had been killed or wounded and that the Huns had attacked from the right where they had crawled along the bed of a creek and gained possession of a large factory, a big two-storey brick building. From this point of vantage they had fired machine guns enfilading the post and killing or wounding all the men who kept their heads up. They had received no support from the post of the Company on my right so I sent the Corporal to see what was wrong. He returned in about ten minutes to say that he had found the garrison of this post just returning to their post, they had been shelled out of it but Lieut. Murdock, their O.C., had sent them back.

I now found Corporal Stewart my Signal Section Corporal had carried out my instructions, issued to him in my prepared Plan of Defence, that in the event of my No. 1 Post being over-run and the enemy breaking through he was to take charge of all the odds and ends attached to my Company Headquarters Staff and with his own Signal Section added, rush them out and occupy a prepared trench that I had got some Tommies to dig the day previously. This post, about 250 yards in front, when and if established, would act as a protection to my Company Headquarters. Stewart had acted immediately on learning of the 'open' front, leaving only the Company Sgt-Major, the Corporal Clerk, some 'Runners' and Stretcher Bearers in occupation of Headquarters.

I at once sent off a note to the Colonel telling him how things stood and went out to see what was going on. I looked about and saw some men moving behind a copse— between Lieut. McGinn's and Lieut. Bourke's posts—and I took them for Bourke's men. Realizing the dangerous situation that had now developed with the destruction of my right post and seeing the rearward movement of McGinn's men commencing to take place from No. 2 Post I called for a runner to take a message to Lieut. Bourke of my No. 3 Post warning him of the situation and instructing him to deploy some of his men to the right to cover McGinn's retirement.

The open warfare nature of the last two day's engagements had proved very exacting on my runners (I had lost two badly wounded) and now found none available. In reply to my calls for a runner a stretcher bearer named Parfrey came forward and volunteered to take my message.

From my point of vantage I watched Parfrey's progress with the greatest anxiety. He had about 500 yards to go and by keeping to the hedges and the edge of the front, taking advantage of all the cover offering, Parfrey reached his destination. I did not see any movement of men in the direction that I wished them to go but plenty of movement and a lot of activity in another direction. It was obvious the Huns were attacking in that direction. Without waiting further I determined to rush out to the new firing line and see what the position was for myself. To get there quickly I ran across the open and was shot at by the Huns from a distance of about 100 yards. On the way I saw Parfrey returning and could see he had something to tell me as he signalled me. I made towards him, he stopped running and opened his mouth to speak and then suddenly collapsed with the words on his lips unspoken. I dropped alongside him to find the blood gushing from a bullet hole in his neck. I tried to stop the flow of blood but found the bullet had made a hole the size of an apple in his throat and that it was hopeless trying to block the flow of blood without choking him, the gash was too big, so leaving him I crawled out the remainder of the distance, 100 yards, to the new post that had been just established by the aid of this gallant stretcher bearer. I found the post well manned and that the men belonged to McGinn's platoon. He had withdrawn his post when his right flank had been turned—the remainder of his men were at that moment digging in on our new line. It was a masterly retirement of McGinn's, brought about with only one casualty, that of Sgt. Short one of the best sergeants in the Battalion. It appears that McGinn, seeing the Huns attack Fenton's post which was on the other side of a small wood and farmhouse, sent a patrol consisting of Sgt. Short and Private 364 J. Dehn, an original Anzac, over to see what was happening. Sgt. Short although hit by a Hun sniper satisfied himself that the post on his right was in possession of the enemy, returned to McGinn (his platoon commander) and told him the situation. McGinn, realizing that he was outflanked and would be cut off then sent Short with a few men to make their way to the rear, 200 yards, and dig another post in rear of the copse that they were defending. Short coolly marked out a trench under machine gun fire and continued working on the trench until being hit a second time by a bullet which shattered his elbow, he was forced reluctantly to go to the rear. Sgt. Short is so badly hurt that he will never do any more soldiering—it is a pity as he would have made a splendid officer. I have made strong recommendation to the Colonel of his gallantry and I think he will get a D.C.M.*

McGinn then withdrew his post, man by man, to their new position. They were hardly there when the Huns overran their old post and commenced working their way down the copse towards our new line. Lieut. Bourke's post then came into the picture and was soon fully engaged in resisting the advancing Germans.

Satisfying myself that all was now well on my left centre I then crawled back to my Headquarters, keeping very low because I was under observation. There I found Signaller Ingamells with my Company Sgt-Major, asking for a stretcher bearer party to bring in L/Cpl. Redmayne, the Company Lewis Gunner who had been badly wounded in the head and appeared blinded.† Ingamells was giving a vivid account

---

* Short got the D.C.M.
† Redmayne was permanently blinded.

of the gallantry of their Reserve Company Gunner who had
been 'collared' by Stewart when he had rushed out to occupy
the new post in front. Ingamells described how they had just
got there in the 'nick of time.' They were hardly in the
trench when the Huns attacked. The ten men spread themselves along the full length of the trench as the Huns came
rushing forward. The small garrison beat them off but the
Hun, reinforced, mounted a second attack preceded by
bombers. This was also beaten off and Ingamells was most
enthusiastic in his praise of Lewis Gunner Redmayne who,
rushing into the far corner of the trench, immediately
opened fire and kept firing. The German attackers soon concentrated their fire upon him but so great was the rapid fire
of the other defenders that the Germans, as usual, retired
out of range.

The promptness of Corporal Stewart in occupying the post
saved the situation and undoubtedly prevented my Headquarters from being over-run. I told Ingamells to congratu-
late Stewart and his men.

I then sent my Corporal Clerk down to see the Colonel
and explain to him the tactical situation. He returned at
the same time as I received a note from the C.O. advising
he had sent Lieut. Johnson with one platoon to reinforce
my left post (Lieut. Pitt) and Lieut. D'Arcy Power with one
platoon was to reinforce McGinn's post and I was to hang
on at all costs. While I was reading the note, in dashed Lieut.
Power—he had left his platoon back in the hedges and had
come on to Company Headquarters to report to me and get
his instructions. He had been told that the Huns had broken
our line and we were nearly all wiped out. At the same time
it appears that Lieut. Johnson dashed up to my left Post
(Pitt) gasping and offered him help only to find there was
nothing doing there, Pitt did not even know we had had a
scrap at all as a big hedge and copse hid us from his view

and over a thousand yards separated him from the right of our line.

I told Power that he could not do better than keep his men where they were until dark, when I would bring them up and post them near McGinn.

We were amused at the state of excitement existing back at Battalion Headquarters. A runner came in soon from B.H.Q. with another alarming note and I obtained from him the reason why. It appears that a Tommy who was on the No. 1 Post that was attacked 'panicked' and rushed down to Battalion Headquarters covered all over with mud and water. He said he had swum down a drain under water and thus escaped—the only man left—and that two of our posts had been wiped out. He said I had sent him so the Colonel naturally believed him. The Colonel of course had to report it at once to Brigade H.Q. with the result that two companies of the 6th Battalion who were in reserve to us moved up to counter-attack and 'dug in' in front of Battalion H.Q. Lieut. Temple, the Intelligence Officer came along and wanted to know if our line 'still held' and all the time we were in our glory except that I was worrying over poor Fenton and had given him up for lost. Suddenly a Tommy came running in with a bandage around his head from a bullet wound to say that he had left Mr Fenton and another Tommy out in a shell hole, still alive. While I was worrying how to get Fenton in as I did not have enough men to counter-attack he and another man suddenly appeared, running across the 100 yards of open ground, shot at by all the Huns who could bring their rifles to bear upon them. I thought they must be hit every yard they went. I happened to be standing at the end of the stone wall at the entrance to my farmhouse with one eye looking round the edge of the stone gate post observing my front and seeing without being seen. When I noticed them I stepped forward and waved, they saw me and changed their direction for the open gate. Huns saw them too and it was miraculous how they escaped being shot as Huns kept shooting at them from the cover of the orchard. Bullets were whizzing by as running and ducking Fenton managed to reach the shelter of the farmhouse accompanied by the faithful Tommy. I couldn't help stepping forward to meet them and grasping Fenton's hand, shook it warmly in my delight at seeing him alive after I had given him up for lost. Turning inside the gate opening they threw themselves down behind the cover of the stone wall gasping for breath, they were just about done.

Fenton told me how he and one Tommy, the sole survivors of his platoon post, had carried out my order—'there was to be no retreat, but to fight it out to the last man.' He told me how the Huns had crept up the creek on his right and bombed his men until they had all become casualties. His platoon sergeant, Sgt. Robertson had done great work with a German machine gun that he had captured, he kept firing towards the attacking Huns advancing on his front until he too was killed. One by one his men, including about 20 Tommies he had taken into his post and who had fought well, had fallen until in the end he and two Tommies were the sole survivors. He told one of the Tommies to make a break for it and report to me at Company Headquarters what had happened. In the meantime he and the other Tommy would cover the man's 'get away' by keeping up firing on the attacking Huns.

This they did and then Fenton told me he said to the remaining Tommy—'Now you go. You see the way your mate went, follow up that ditch along the road keeping under cover until you reach the orchard and then run for it.' 'And what will you do?' asked the Tommy. 'Well, I will keep firing to keep the Huns back.' 'I won't leave you,' the Tommy replied. 'Well,' said Fenton, 'we will go together' and this they did. As they made their way towards Company Headquarters they found Huns in front of them also creeping forward. Some of these they shot as they overtook them and whilst crawling along, in front of them they spotted a Hun climbing up a ladder on the safety side of a haystack the better able to observe my Headquarters. They shot the Hun who had his back towards them and then having reached the corner of the orchard, they both made a dash for it.

I sent Fenton off to rest in one of the bedrooms in the farmhouse and told him not to show himself for the rest of the day.

I then again crawled out to McGinn's post to see if he was alright and inform him of my new dispositions. He was in great spirits and his platoon had suffered only seven casualties, all wounded. He told me I was lucky to have got out to his post as Hun snipers were in position only 50 yards away in front in a small copse.

Talking to Lieut. Power after he had reported to me I obtained an account of the wonderful defence put up by my No. 1 Post. Power told me walking wounded who passed through rear Battalion Headquarters on the way to the Dressing Station had all talked about it and of the admiration they had for their Platoon Commander, Lieut. Fenton who steadied the men until one by one all became casualties and then, like the Captain of a ship remained on deck to the last. Power was relieved to know that Fenton had survived and was well. Many mentioned Sgt. Robertson's bravery, Power said they kept talking about it and thought he (Robertson) should receive a posthumous V.C.

After Fenton had rested and had a good sleep I asked him for his report. He spoke highly of the conduct of all his N.C.O's. and their bravery and devotion to duty, particularly praising Corporal Rainbow, 3960, killed; Corporal Whelan, 2822, wounded and then missing; Corporal G. P. White, 4225, wounded and Corporal R. Hill, wounded but carrying on. In the early part of the defence they all showed outstanding gallantry and initiative, mostly in reconnaissance and observation work and later as junior leaders in the control of their men during the withdrawal of the platoon to its alternative position. Sergeant Robertson with his captured German machine gun stayed behind and covered the retirement of the platoon to their new post in the rear, holding back the enemy who were advancing in large numbers throwing bombs, he stuck to his post until he fell.

When I asked Fenton about the men's talk of Robertson earning a V.C. he replied, 'There were so many that deserved one it was difficult to differentiate,' but what did distinguish him was that when the Company moved off from Hazebrouck Railway Station Robertson was detailed to remain behind with the nucleus and I was unaware that he had not done so until I heard that he was in the front line. Robertson had followed up and joined us whilst we were advancing through Nieppe Forest saying, 'I couldn't bear to stay behind and miss out on this great occasion! I want to be with my platoon.' When Fenton had told me this earlier it was too late for me to order Robertson back, particularly as his Platoon Commander was loath to report him for he was already engaged in fighting, so I let it go. Although he sacrificed his life his action in holding back the enemy as he did undoubtedly saved many of his wounded comrades who were able to crawl away to the rear and find their way to the Field Ambulance but, as has been said, there were so many deserving of the highest decoration.

When night came I got Power with his platoon and took them out to place them in position filling a nasty bend in my line caused by the loss of Fenton's post and McGinn's withdrawal. On the way I found two men from my left post who had heard nothing of McGinn's post having withdrawn (they were too far away to see) and they had called in on the way down to my C.H.Q. to see their mates in McGinn's post. To their utter surprise they found the post deserted. They looked around and made no endeavour to keep quiet.

Finding no-one they had made over to the next post, Bourke's, to tell him of their discovery. On hearing the lads' story I decided to send Power with his platoon to seize the bridgehead over the canal leading to this post and to let the Colonel know at once in case he contemplated counter-attacking to get the two lost posts back again. Realizing Power was unfamiliar with the terrain I accompanied the platoon out myself and posted them over the bridgehead. We found no Huns or any sign of them so I immediately returned and sent off a runner to the C.O. telling him what I had done and asking for instructions. Word came back that there was to be no counter-attack so I went out to withdraw the men from their lonely vigil.

When I reached the bridgehead I found all the men sound asleep, they were so over-tired with all their travelling and marching that they could not stay awake. Each man I went to was lying in the same position, face downwards with his rifle out in front of him and I had to go along and slap every man to make him wake up. (These men were part of the company we had left behind in Amiens to follow on· in a later train.) I then withdrew them to our main line and placed them in positions where they could give a good account of themselves if the Hun should attack. With this added strength to my command I now felt my position so secure that I had no need for further worry about my inadequate defence line. By the time I had done this dawn was breaking and I had just time to get back to my farmhouse without being observed by the enemy. I found poor old Fenton still lying on a bed fast asleep, dead to the world after his exciting and nerve racking experiences of the previous day.

The C.O. had asked for artillery to blow the factory right off the map, which the Artillery Liaison Officer had promised to do, so we waited expectantly for our guns to open up but it was eleven o'clock before they commenced shooting at the factory. I was so dog-tired after breakfast I took off my boots and chose one of the nice feathered beds with snow white sheets and 'turned in.' Everything was now quiet—the enemy had settled down to working out plans how he could dislodge us from our strong positions—and not a shot was being fired by either side. How quiet everything seemed now and what a lot of exciting things had happened the last week, or was it only a day! In my tired mind I could not determine whether it was the previous night, or two nights ago that the Tommies had been over-running my comfortable Headquarters. I remembered one scene about midnight when I had several Commanding Officers and their staffs in my dining room, all seated on chairs round the fire, lamenting the loss of their battalions and the beastly show they had put up. My batman reminded me that I had had nothing to eat since lunch and laid the table and placed my dinner in front of me. It was certainly a most fashionable hour, midnight or over to dine off poultry. I invited the English officers to join me in helping to demolish a boiled fowl but only one, a Major, availed himself of my invitation. I think they were all too ashamed of the situation to accept the hospitality of a mere Lieutenant and an Australian at that.

One by one they disappeared off into space until by morning only one of them was left and he was fast asleep. Where they all went I don't know but I imagine they made their way to the rear and picked up their Brigade H.Q. somewhere or other and reported themselves to their General. The officer lying asleep I then recognised as the Intelligence Officer of the 1st Lancashire Fusiliers, 29th Division. He was a real soldier, one of the good ones of the old school. . . Yes, I thought to myself as I lay on my bed too over-tired to fall asleep, that scene was not last night but two nights ago—or was it some picture I had seen of war as it used to be when I was a boy—and I was only imagining that the scene of the midnight dinner with the English Major was real. No it was not real, I must have been dreaming, for was I not lying on a soft bed in some English country house? I must be on leave!

I was awakened about two o'clock in the afternoon by hearing the sound of heavy artillery firing. The big shells were bursting close handy and the ground shook with the force of the detonation of the shells as they struck the ground. I called for my Boy (Newman) who told me that our Artillery was trying to blow down the factory but were making very bad shooting. The heavy guns had commenced shooting at eleven o'clock in the morning and had dropped shells very short, some falling very near our foremost posts. The Artillery Liaison officers were at my Headquarters observing and my second-in-command, Lieut. Stevenson had spent the whole of the time at the telephone ringing up the artillery to increase their range.

My Boy brought me a fried egg for lunch so I turned over as soon as I had eaten it and went off to sleep leaving the correction of the guns to the officers already attending to the matter. At four o'clock I arose and went out to see what damage had been done to the factory. I found the artillery had just secured their first hit and were busy pounding the factory to pieces now that they had secured the correct elevation. Huns were running in all directions from the factory which soon caught on fire and burnt brilliantly. The Church at Vieux Berquin was also being shelled by our gunners as the Huns were using the steeple as an O.P. and a machine gun post. 18-pounder shells had secured direct hits time after time in the face of the clock and soon a heavy gun completed the demolition of the tower by placing a shell right at the base of the steeple which caused it to collapse. It was terrible to watch the destruction of this pretty little village church in the centre of the square by our own guns but it was a military necessity. The Huns were looking down on us and our lines from the splendid view obtained from this vantage point. In addition, they were using the Village Square as an assembly point. When the steeple at last collapsed our boys were so glad they could hardly restrain a cheer. A man came running in at this minute to say that Mr. McGinn had been wounded by one of our own shells. I sent him back to find out if it was necessary to have him carried in at once by stretcher bearers. If so he was to wave his hand back to me. I watched him run out again to the post across the hundred yards of open field. He was sniped at but not hit and reached the post safely. He shook his head back at me to signify that there was no need for stretcher bearers. Later I found out it was a big piece of earth that had hit McGinn on the side of his head, turning up his hard steel helmet on one side like an Australian hat, but not doing any more harm than badly bruising his face and neck.

Capt. Lodge, the Adjutant then looked me up to find out my new dispositions and the steps I had taken for the defence of my sector. He was very satisfied with all that he saw and seemed quite pleased with the position. I took the opportunity of enlarging on the fatigue of my men for allowing a suspected German spy to escape, letting him know how badly in want of rest and how absolutely done all my men were. I related to him the extraordinary experience of the night before, or rather the early morning when at about four o'clock my right post heard a man riding a bicycle down the road from the direction of the rear of our lines, they called out to him to halt but the man increased his pace and made a bolt for it. He ran into the barricade of old farm waggons across the road, dismounted and throwing his bike over, scrambled after it. The Lewis guns opened fire on him but without effect and this spy, for such he assuredly was, got away scot free. He must have been one of the many Germans that came through our lines during the retreat dressed as refugees. I saw several of these fellows myself actually entering our lines under shell fire from the Huns and at the time pitied them—they were dressed as old men and women. I took the responsibility myself of having let this man escape, I would not charge my sentries with carelessness as I knew how absolutely dog-tired and worn out they all were. I told the Adjutant that he would now know the condition of the men and what they were enduring.

Just as I was about to set out on my rounds after dark the C.O. rang up and asked me how my defences were and if I needed any more help to repel a threatened Hun attack. I told him of my right flank so he offered me another platoon which I accepted. This platoon reported under Lieut. Dowling about eleven o'clock and by daylight next morning they had dug themselves in on the inside of a hedge with a Lewis gun covering my right flank. Also, the C.O. sent another platoon with two Lewis guns under Lieut. Johnston, to dig in on a line between my two left posts covering a possible crossing in the canal which ran across my company sector front. After this I felt doubly sure of my ability to withstand any attack the Hun might make upon us. The night passed quietly. Next day when the main enemy attack did develop it was on our left Brigade front and was held.

16th April 1918

A communication from Battalion said Brigade had asked for enemy identification and could I catch a 'live' Hun. An easy enough request or order whichever way you look at it, but not so easy to carry out. The normal method would be a raiding party under an officer but in my position I had no spare officer or enough men to carry out such a job.

I put the matter to a stretcher bearer, Morgan, a man who was always ready for an adventurous job quite outside his normal work of picking up wounded men and carrying them in on a stretcher, very often under heavy machine gun fire. This stretcher job alone was dangerous enough to satisfy an ordinary man, but Morgan was no ordinary man. He was a character known throughout the whole Battalion—not only his Company—and like some diggers, was no good on parade or behind the Line. When an inspection by a Senior Officer was about to take place his Company Commander would see that Morgan did not appear, he was hidden away somewhere out of sight because he was always dirtily turned out, boots unpolished, tunic torn, hat turned up at the wrong angle and altogether most unsoldierly in appearance but when in the Line, was truly wonderful and worth half a dozen ordinary men for his initiative and bravery.

I called him up and spoke to him. 'Morgan,' I said, 'I want you to go out and catch a live Hun and bring him in. We want identification of what German Units are opposing us, that's the main job. If no live Huns are about, search the ground for dead German officers and see if they have any papers on them that will give us the information we want,' and off he went—it was two o'clock in the morning. He returned in about an hour, covered in mud and his pockets bulging with maps and papers he had collected. He reported, 'I couldn't see any live Huns but lots of German dead lying about and from a dead German officer I got a big automatic revolver and several maps and plans.' I sent all the papers straight down to Battalion Headquarters and shortly afterwards the Adjutant rang and said 'All correct, splendid.'

The day passed in quietness. Lieut. Woodhouse, an acting Company Commander, came up in the afternoon to look around as the C.O. had decided to divide the sector I held into two Company sectors instead of one. As soon as it was dark we reshuffled the platoons a bit and all 'A' Company came to the right and all 'D' Company to the left. I handed over my nice comfortable farmhouse to Woodhouse and withdrew. While I was attending to this relief I sent Lieut. Stevenson and the Company Sgt.-Major to make their way over to the left of the Battalion area and choose another Company Headquarters. When I left my old Headquarters it was one o'clock in the morning and I was so tired I could hardly drag my legs after me but I did not forget to take with me the gramophone that my batman had found in the farmhouse and which we played whenever the Huns commenced shelling. We could only find five records and these same records we played and played, over and over again. They were all pretty French dance tunes, mostly Quadrilles.

17th April 1918

By the time we were re-established in the new farmhouse chosen as our new C.H.Q. it was nearly dawn. The place ordered by the Colonel for us to go to was 600 yards behind the Front Line, in a lot of trees and hedges so I was quite out of touch with my posts. I could see none of them, so had to do without a Company O.P. About nine o'clock the Huns put over a most intense 5.9 barrage on our support lines, concentrating on 'B' Company's headquarters and on their support posts, but missing my H.Q. The shells burst in dozens on either side of us leaving a gap of 100 yards on each side. I got the men up (they had all chosen the best places they could find and gone off to sleep) and made them scatter about and lie down. Corporal Hill, already wounded but carrying on, was again wounded in the back by a shell splinter. He was standing up at the time and the piece came from a shell which burst nearly 100 yards away. My telephone line was cut so I sent a signaller out along the line to find the break and mend it. When half an hour passed and he had not returned I sent out two more signallers to run the wire out and see if they could find trace of the first signaller. They returned in a few minutes with a wounded man they had picked up. The man was badly hurt in the head and belonged to 'B' Company. The signallers reported the line badly broken in dozens of places where it crossed the road so I gave up the attempt to mend it. I went out shortly afterwards to look about and found Capt. Lovett, O.C. 'B'

Company with a bandage on his jaw—a piece of shell had knocked his front teeth out—and he told me he had retained my signaller in his trenches and that he was safe. Gas shells were falling in the vicinity and I got a mouthful before I could get my gas helmet on.

About midday the bombardment eased off and gradually died out. My own Company had only suffered the one casualty, Cpl. Hill, wounded—the bombardment had not touched my front posts. However, 'B' Company had 'caught' it pretty hot. Capt. Lovett was killed, also Sgt. Gunn D.C.M. (my old platoon sergeant of No. 5 Platoon, 'B' Company) who had been with me in the big fighting of last autumn at Polygon Wood and Broadseinde Ridge. 'B' Company was to have relieved my Company in the front line that night but owing to the loss of their O.C. and the many casualties they had suffered I had to hang on for another day and night.

When it was dark enough I was soon hastening up to the front line to enquire how my posts had survived the ordeal and was gratified to find they had only suffered two men killed, both on Lieut. Pitt's post. I got Lieut. Fenton to relieve Lieut. McGinn so that McGinn could have a few hours sleep in at C.H.Q., but before leaving I got him to send a patrol out to patrol our front and try and find out the position of the enemies posts on our immediate front. The patrol returned at 12.30 a.m. and reported that they had found no Huns this side of the small canal. I then went along with some men to 'A' Company H.Q., my old home, and got a lot of blankets and overcoats, corn sacks, etc. for Lieut. Bourke's post. The cold was intense and the men were suffering terribly. When I returned back to my H.Q. I found an officer and five N.C.O's. of the 6th Battalion who had come up with word that their Battalion was going to relieve us the following night and the N.C.O's. were to spend the day on the posts. I had just time to send them out with the breakfast rations before morning broke. Owing to the many changes and the different platoons I had had in my command the rations had not been at all satisfactory—generally a shortage every morning. Had it not been for the food we managed to salvage from farms we would have been in a very bad way.

18th April 1918

About midday I received the operation order for our relief by the 6th Battalion between 8 o'clock and midnight the coming night. At four o'clock a buzz came on the 'phone and the Adjutant told me Battalion Order No. 29 was cancelled. This prepared me for the information which reached me by runner soon afterwards that an enemy attack was expected to take place within the next 24 hours on our front and that we had to stay in to resist the attack. The officer and N.C.O's. of the 6th Battalion had to report back to their battalion as soon as it was possible for the N.C.O's. to be withdrawn from the front line. Later on word reached us that a prisoner had been captured by the 7th Battalion and he had given the information of the impending attack. I sent to the dump of S.A.A. that we had found just behind our front line and placed an additional four boxes of ammunition on all my posts as well as two boxes of rifle grenades. I inspected the Line about midnight to see for myself if all orders were understood by my platoon commanders. I visited Lieut. Evans, a boy who had come to our battalion from 1st Division Pioneers only a few months ago and I have never seen a boy more cheery or more anxious for a fight than he was. I took my bugler and a stretcher bearer along with me. The former carrying a basin of hot stew for Evan's men who, owing to a blunder had not had any hot rations sent up to them. The stretcher bearer Morgan carried a couple of boxes of rifle grenades and I carried an armful of flares for obtaining contact with aeroplanes. I also brought a handful of 'Very' lights. After a chat with Evans I went along and had a yarn to the Company Commander of the 2nd Battalion which was on my left. While there a message came along to the effect that the intended enemy attack was to take place at five o'clock in the morning, so 'cheerio to five o'clock' became my farewell to all my platoon commanders as I went the rounds satisfying myself that everything was in order and that the men all knew what to expect. I returned to my Headquarters leaving the men in the Front Line in the best of spirits. The men were eager for a fight, confident that they could hold their ground. All the posts were crammed with boxes of S.A.A. and they would have been good Huns that could have broken our line that morning.

Five o'clock found me on the road leading from my C.H.Q. to the outpost line. Hatless and without a respirator I was on a high piece of ground overlooking the front line where I could see any attack develop. At ten minutes to the hour all our Artillery opened on the enemy's trenches along the whole line. The hour came and passed, snow had fallen during the early hours of morning and the ground was covered white showing up the slightest movement—it was an ideal morning to resist an attack. I was never so confident that we would give a good account of ourselves. I felt the drawback of being a Company Commander. Here was I sitting back with nothing to do but to wait and watch. At that moment I would much sooner have taken my place as a platoon commander in one of the outposts and taken my chance. As I looked across the open flat country I could see nearly all the front line but not pick out any of the posts, they were so well camouflaged by the snow. Not a movement could be seen anywhere over the wide expanse of country, to all intent the country was deserted.

Away on the right in 'C' Company area I suddenly saw a man appear walking from a farmhouse behind 'C' Company Headquarters and deliberately walk out a hundred yards to an advanced post where he jumped in and disappeared from sight. How foolish, I thought, a dozen Hun observers must have noticed the movement and thus knew of the otherwise hidden post with the result that the enemy artillery would know where to shell. As no enemy attack eventuated our artillery gradually slackened down until it ceased altogether and I returned to my farm feeling a bit disappointed that there had been no Hun attack. I had arranged everything so nicely to give the Hun a very warm reception. I think the majority of my Company were as disappointed as I was myself.

As soon as I had had my breakfast I turned in and slept until I was awakened by my Sergeant Major who told me that an officer of the 31st Division was there to see me. This Division had been reorganized and made up to strength by new drafts of young lads and officers from England who were taking over from us that night. I was as nice to him as I could be under the circumstances, considering I had had no sleep the night before or the night before that and so on for the last week. I gave him all the information he wanted about how I held the Line, my arrangements for rations, the dispositions and orders in case of attack, etc., wrote out my defence scheme for him and then, after he had taken up over an hour of my precious sleep he left me. I again turned in to be awakened about three o'clock by another officer, a Captain who told me that his company was going to relieve under different arrangements—two battalions were going to relieve our one (a not unusual thing at that time) so I had to set to again and go all over the old business of handing over an area of the defence line to a new unit, but I easily satisfied this Captain. I don't think he had ever been in the Line before—from his questions and manner he struck me as a great 'dud.' He did not even know how to fire the S.O.S. rocket off. I promised to show him but forgot to and was jolly glad afterwards for forgetting. It was a crying shame to put men like him in charge of 200 human lives (the strength of an English Company). About double our own.

I suggested to the captain that as soon as it was a little darker and the Huns could not see us, I would take him along my Company front and point out salient features—the weak spots in our defence and if the enemy attacked, where he would have to be prepared to reinforce that position. No, he said, he wouldn't go—that was not his job. He would leave it to his second-in-command. His place was to remain at Company Headquarters and fight his Company from there! He complained that the position of my Company Headquarters was too near the front line—it should be at least 1000 yards in rear of the forward posts as the Text Books said, whereas I had placed it only 600 yards behind the forward posts. The Text Book also laid down, etc., etc. . . I had to let it go at that, I never attempted to tell him any more, he knew everything. I didn't even bother to tell him we Australians ran things differently regarding our second-in-command of Companies who stayed behind at the waggon lines in Reserve, to be ready to take over Command of the Company in the event of its O.C. becoming a casualty and as Company Commander I preferred to be in close touch with my platoon commanders instead of out of touch.

He was also very critical about my farmhouse cooking arrangements. As we stood at the door of the farm the Company cook passed through carrying a dixie of boiled potatoes—he walked fully twenty yards away to a hedge where he drained off the water and then returned to the kitchen to repeat the performance—and what a lot of abuse the English Captain then gave vent to. He had always been told what an undisciplined lot the Australians were and now here was proof of it. Why hadn't I constructed proper grease traps as instructed in the Manual of Field Training—Cooking Arrangements for Bivouac Camps! I really now got impatient with him and didn't waste my time in telling him we had only occupied the farm the day previously and expected the building to be blown to bits as soon as the Huns discovered we were occupying the place as a Headquarters!

At 8.30 p.m. the first of the relieving platoons turned up and were led by my waiting guides out to their positions. The new Company Headquarters staff now took over and I left the new outfit in position and moved out with my batman and the remainder of my own staff reporting 'Relief OK' at forward Battalion Headquarters.

As I passed along the road I met Paddy Bourke with his platoon, all eating the hot potatoes which I had ordered to be cooked in their jackets and placed in dixies on the road so that as the 'relieved' men passed by on the way out each man could pick up a hot potato—the only food they would get until next morning when they would reach the 'Waggon Lines.'

At Battalion Headquarters I met my friend the Major with whom I had had the argument over the map when he was rallying the demoralized Tommies on the afternoon of the 13th. We had a good laugh over the incident of the shot that was fired at us which killed the calf. He was the new C.O. of the relieving English Battalion. Everyone was in a jolly mood and we all shook hands and left each other the best of friends. I wished him luck with his new command— I felt he needed encouragement. All my platoon commanders had critical things to say about their relieving English opposite numbers who seemed to have no idea of where their platoon front should begin and end and the men seemingly had no confidence in their leaders. All seemed bewildered at the proceedings, as happened once before in our experience, some even started lining the back of the trench instead of the parapet, looking inwards instead of outwards.

From the Line we marched to Borre Huts about 7 kilos away. On the way I picked up my company with the S.M. leading the goat he had salvaged, or rather the goat was leading him, trotting ahead as proud as punch of his new owners. I carried out the gramophone I had salvaged. It just fitted into a pack which I carried on my back and I gave the funnel to the bugler to carry. I am hopeful of getting it with its five records out to Australia, it will make an interesting souvenir.

On reaching Borre I reported to the Colonel and told him how well all my officers had behaved and he said they had done splendidly. I particularly praised the work of Lieutenants Fenton and McGinn in the anticipation that these exceptionally gallant officers would receive decorations. I also recommended a number of men for decorations including Sergeant Short, Corporals White and Stewart and two stretcher bearers, also Corporal Rainbow and two others— (most of them obtained military medals, but not a single officer was given an award).*

After resting at Borre for two days the battalion got orders to go into support trenches to the 5th and 6th battalions who were in the Line. I was told to remain in charge of the company, but Lieutenant Findlay who had returned from the training battalion in England and whom the C.O. had detailed as Second-in-Command to me, was found to be so senior that at the last minute the Colonel decided that I should stay out in reserve and Captain Campbell should take the company in. I was very disappointed at not going into the Line again but realised that a rest would do me no harm.

27th April 1918

After a week in the reserve unit—which was an organized Company with Major Traill in Command, Blackman as Second-in-Command, two other officers and myself as platoon commanders—I suddenly got orders at 12 o'clock to report to the 1st Australian Divisional Wing, 15th Corps Reinforcement Camp, Linghem—a back area about 20 miles behind

---

* An officer's decoration meant a citation would be published.

the Front Line in a peaceful part of the country where reinforcements from England were received before being drafted to their battalions.

Major Traill went to the telephone and the C.O. told him I had to go as a Lewis gun instructor. I knew nothing about Lewis guns but I was told that 'I must be a Lewis gun instructor.' I was to report to Lieut. Carne at Rear Div. H.Q. at noon the following day, I had earned a rest in a 'Back Area.'

Postscript: the German point of view

Some of the reactions of the Germans to their defeat at Nieppe Forest are recorded by Bean.

> German records make it plain that the battle of April 14—the first day of fighting for the Australians engaged —was for the Germans the third day of a stubborn battle in which progress had been . . . disappointing . . . The original instructions given by the Crown Prince Rupprecht to the [German] Sixth Army had 'laid it down as a condition of success that . . . on the second day the chain of heights [from Kemmell westwards] should already be attained'. He had even hoped that in the first few days the Sixth Army, following up the beaten enemy, might break through the St. Omer defences before British reinforcements could arrive from the south . . . Progress had dropped far behind these expectations, but yet had been fast enough to make it possible on April 12th that Hazebrouck or the chain of hills, or both, might be reached . . . The 35th [German] Division, pushing towards the north-east corner of Nieppe Forest, came . . . 'against strong opposition' [that of the 4th Guards Brigade] . . . 'Vieux Berquin was the scene of heavy fighting' (against the 29 Division) . . . [To the south of Nieppe Forest the British (5th Division) were holding whilst in the north, strong opposition was met, (Scottish troops and a New Zealand force made up of a New Zealand Entrenching Battalion, who turned

themselves into infantry, did a magnificent job until re-lieved by French reinforcements). But it was the defence of Nieppe Forest that halted the German advance. German history records state that their 15th Corps after heavy fighting succeeded in getting into the edge of Nieppe Forest (but the statement is not correct—the forest was held by the 2nd Australian Brigade) .]

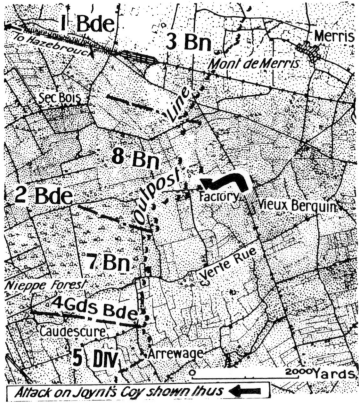

Source: Australian War Memorial

'The opposition of the enemy,' the *Reichsarchiv* states, 'was everywhere extremely stubborn. He defended himself especially by means of skilfully built machine-gun nests which could only be spotted at the last moment.'*

*This was exactly what I hoped would happen when I earlier had the argument with the English Major who said he couldn't see my posts.

The front of the XIX [German] Corps was now of practically the same length as that of the 1st Australian Division ... 'But the enemy is a tough one,' says the [German] historian ... 'In cleverly built up machine-gun nests he flanks the infantry, especially from Strazeele station and Nieppe Forest.' As usual, German batteries accompanied the infantry ... a section of the 5th Battery, supporting the infantry, managed to blow out two Australian posts [probably those of Fenton and McGinn] ...

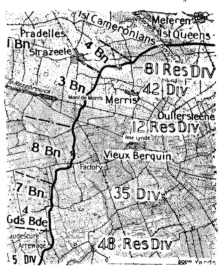

Source: Australian War Memorial

But ... when its two leading regiments attacked, there met them from all the windows of Caudescure, just outside the forest, such a hail of small arms fire that the attack came to a stop with heavy losses.

For the first time on the main front of the offensive, hardly any ground had been gained. The completeness of the defeat was not recognized at first; Crown Prince Rupprecht says that 'in the course of the afternoon there came in an order, this time personally signed by Hindenburg, which ... urged the Sixth Army to push on ... The Kaiser, who called at Headquarters of the Sixth Army, spoke in the same way. 'But,' adds Rupprecht, 'of what use are any number of orders to attack if the troops have no longer the power to do so? . . . The C.G.S. of the Sixth Army expressed himself most pessimistically—the attack had to all appearances run to a standstill.'*

An Australian division consisted of twelve infantry battalions plus artillery, engineers, a machine gun battalion and a pioneer battalion. It originally held about 20,000 men but by 1917, after losses, was only about half-strength, its fighting strength being about 9,000 men at most. A German division was about 12,000 so the 1st Australian Division of 9,000 men opposed a German force of 50,000 men.

Diary continues: 28th April 1918

The following morning saw me with my batman and my valise in the officer's mess cart driving along the Hazebrouck Road to Eblinghem, a journey of 12 kilos. From there I picked up Carne, who was also being sent down to the camp as Musketry instructor, together with three N.C.O's. I had lunch with Carne at the Div. Mess and then we journeyed to our destination first by 'hopping' motor lorries and then 'jumping' a supply train which took us down the line to Berquette where we had a walk of 5 miles out to the camp at Linghem which we reached at 8 o'clock. Mess was formal so we waited until after mess when we were part of a second sitting of officers. After Mess we reported to Major Ayris the O.C. of the Wing who received us and showed us off to our quarters.

The reinforcement camp was a Tommy camp. However, we found the camp most enjoyable with a splendid Mess, only costing 21 francs a week. A first-rate concert party played every night and soon after getting there we got a cricket team going and had quite a large amount of cricket during the next six weeks that we stayed there. Our work was very interesting. All men returning to their units from hospital

* Bean, *Official History . . .*, vol. v, pp. 474-8.

were given a few hours instruction in the practical use of the Lewis gun and also some musketry practice on the range. Some days there were no drafts in so I had plenty of time off for recreation. There were some delightful walks in the neighbourhood of the camp and what with cricket, concerts and other entertainments, I managed to have a most enjoyable time. I met many English and Scottish officers and had some very interesting conversations with them. Numbers of our own officers passed through the camp on their way back to their battalions so I met quite a number of old friends.

Among the men passing through were drafts of young English recruits aged only eighteen years. Lloyd George was emptying the camps in England and sending them over to France to build up the re-formed English Divisions that had suffered so severely in the recent Hun offensive. Many of these men had never handled a rifle, or even seen a Lewis gun. They were in the camp for twenty-four hours. Our job was to instruct them in the use of these arms all the morning and in the afternoon they practised field firing on an adjacent rifle range. After that they were sent forward to join the Regiments and Battalions they had been allotted to. I was given nine Tommy sergeant instructors, experts on the Lewis gun. I liked the sergeants and at our morning 'smoko' used to get them talking and obtain their views on things and occasionally I gave them my views too. Once I said to them, 'You know, I am happier here with you sergeants than I am in your Officer's Mess.' Immediately there was a chorus from the sergeants, 'Because our officers are jealous of you Australians, that's why Sir!'

7th June 1918

And now, after nearly six weeks, I find the job I came to do completed as the camp is breaking up into a number of small Divisional Camps at each Divisional railhead so we are all returning back to our units.

Postscript: General Birdwood takes over command of the New Army and General Monash becomes G.O.C. the Australian Corps

In June we got the information that at last all Australian divisions were to come under one Command—all, that is, except ours, the 1st, which would remain temporarily in Flanders as the Second Army Commander, General Plumer, refused to let us go until the defence of Hazebrouck was more secure. We further learnt that the Fifth Army, which was virtually destroyed by the big German offensive in March, was being reformed. Its Commander, General Gough, had been dismissed and sent home—and the new Fifth Army command was being given to General Birdwood, who had taken his Chief of Staff, General Sir Brudenell White with him. General Monash, commanding our 3rd Division, had been appointed G.O.C. Australian Corps with Brigadier-General Blamey as his Chief of Staff.

We admired Birdwood and were sorry to see him go. We did not know Monash so did not have the same affection for him as we had for Birdwood, nor did we of the older divisions think much of the 3rd Division that he commanded. This division was the last Australian one to be formed. It was created in Australia and had missed Gallipoli, the Somme offensive and the terrible winter on the Somme in 1916-17. Consequently the older Australian divisions looked upon the 3rd as 'new chums'. However, a remarkable change of opinion came over us all in the 1st Division when we heard from the officers of the British division that had come up from the Somme and relieved us after Nieppe Forest, how well the 3rd Division had done in stopping the Huns opposite Amiens, and what a name that division had made for Australia. From this moment we accepted them as our equals and were proud to have General Monash as the leader of what was now virtually the Australian Army — though not in name. The British High Command would not agree to the Australian Corps being called an Army because under its ruling an Army had to consist of six or more divisions.

We were not at all sorry to see General Gough go. Australian troops had suffered much by his mishandling of them, particularly after the battle of Pozières and during the Somme winter of 1916-17. He had used the Australian divisions far more than other British divisions to make limited attacks on narrow fronts. In forty-five days he launched nineteen attacks by Australians—sixteen at night —and they held every enemy trench once captured. After losing 17,000 men in their first tour at Pozières Australian divisions were again given an impossible task—to drive a further wedge behind Thiepval where British divisions had failed to make progress. This cost 6,300 casualties and produced no useful result: it merely embittered the troops, who knew they had been mishandled. Birdwood notwithstanding his popularity, came under severe criticism for allowing us to be treated differently from other British divisions. During these eight weeks of piecemeal attacks there was only one sector on that front where British forces steadily pushed ahead, and that was at Pozières, *our* front. But it was on that mile of summit that the three Australian divisions lost 23,000 officers and men and we blamed Gough for that.

Furthermore, by driving into the enemy's line on narrow fronts the troops were put in untenable positions, which allowed them to be enfiladed from both sides; and by hanging on without the neighbouring British divisions coming up on either side, they suffered heavy casualties without gain.

In spite of these severe losses the morale of the Australian troops always remained high. At the first Battle of Pozières in July 1916 I, with others, was left out in the nucleus.

Pozières was a night attack and next morning an order arrived for all officers in the nucleus to report to their battalions. When I did so I was informed that the 8th Battalion was digging in 200 yards in front of the village that they had captured. I, a 2nd Lieutenant, was told to take over 'A' Company and was led out by a 'runner' to where they were.

It was my first experience of front line fighting.

I found the remnants of the company lining shell holes facing the enemy; the trench that they had dug had been obliterated by German shell fire and all the officers in the company had become casualties, as had the Company Sergeant Major and every N.C.O. except one, a sergeant. German shells were falling all around. One burst close by just after I had jumped into a shell hole and as I was talking to the Sergeant. He went to investigate and came back saying, 'Three more gone, only fifteen of us left now' (out of a strength the night before of 150 o/ranks and five officers).

Shortly after, a messenger arrived to say that a large force of Germans was assembling to make an attack, which they did. The remnants, with no thought of retiring from the impossible position they were in (fifteen men on a 200-yard front), immediately climbed out of their shell holes, lined the edges and began shooting at the advancing Germans, who went to ground. We held on there for two days and at midnight were relieved by a full company of nearly 200 men of the 2nd Division, who kept running all over the place looking for the trench they were told we were occupying so that they could jump in and get cover from the fusillade of shells that were falling all round.

In handing over my company front all I could say to the Company Commander relieving me was, 'There is your front, I don't know where our flanks are—good luck.' And scrambling out of the shell hole I was occupying I told the Sergeant to lead the way. Following last, we set off at a run to get clear of the enemy artillery barrage.

After running for about ten minutes I suddenly found the head of our drawn-out line catching up on me from behind. Because of the intense shell fire it was difficult to keep direction, and we had been running in a circle. I just yelled 'about turn' and led the party myself to our destination, a huge chalk pit about a mile to the rear of our front line where we threw ourselves down, exhausted. But we were clear of the shells. My batman alongside me started groaning: 'Take my boot off, I have sprained my ankle.' When I started to do so I found his ankle had swollen so much that I could not get the boot free and had to cut it away with a knife. 'When did this happen?' I asked him. 'Just as we were scrambling out of the shell hole,' he replied. And yet, so great was the fury of hell behind us that he had run all the way alongside me on his injured foot!

After a three-hour rest there the battalion, or what was left of it, reassembled and at daybreak marched to a rest camp a day's march away, myself leading all that remained of 'A' Company. We were all half-dazed and in a sort of stupor with weariness and fatigue and shell shock.

After only two weeks of rest, during which time we were built up to full strength again by brand-new drafts of reinforcements from the depots, we were sent in to the Second Battle of Pozières, and the battalion was once more nearly decimated by heavy casualties.

For the next nine months the A.I.F. divisions in turn were continually in the line fighting battle after battle, enduring the horrors of the 1916 winter in the mud among the shell holes filled with water.

During this time Gough had the Australian divisions hammering away at the German strongholds, fighting battle after battle until the spring came and the Huns retreated to the first of their 'Hindenberg Lines'.

Then came the major battle of Lagnicourt and Bullecourt in April and May—a total of nine months of continuous

fighting without relief before Gough was persuaded by representation, in writing, from Birdwood and General White,
his Chief of Staff, to withdraw the five Australian divisions
for a three-month rest period.

C.E.W. Bean commented on the operations of this time:

> In those forty-five days Australians had launched nineteen
> attacks—all except two being on a narrow front, and
> sixteen at night. They knew their constant advances during
> a time of deadlock would compare with any other achieve-
> ment on the Somme. Under bombardment, of intensity
> and duration probably unsurpassed, they had held every
> trench once firmly captured. But they felt little confidence
> in the high tactics and strategy of it all. Indeed not a few
> British and oversea divisions that served there under
> Gough dreaded ever again to experience the results of his
> optimistic tactical aims and his urgency when caution
> was needed.*

After our withdrawal from the Fifth Army, when we went
up north into Flanders, we never fought again in that Army
until March and April 1918, when we went to it as rescuers.

We had no complaints about other British Army Generals,
only Gough. We respected Plumer of the Second Army under
whom we fought throughout the terrible battles of 1917
and the terrific Passchendaele operations.

It turned out that this three months respite we had now
been given was also to prepare us for taking part in the Passchendaele operations, which lasted four months. At the end
of this break we were in fine fettle.

Criticism by English writers that the Australian Forces
had a bigger percentage of deserters than any of the other
dominions is hard to believe. During the whole of the war
I personally only knew of one case where a Digger dropped
back by falling behind as we were moving up to attack. He
was immediately arrested and, charged later with desertion,

* C.E.W. Bean, *Anzac to Amiens* (Sydney, 1946), p. 264.

was given two years penal servitude, although the poor chap was a bundle of nerves and just couldn't face the Hun any more. The A.I.F. as a whole always retained its high morale and willingness—again and again, without hesitation—to continue fighting.

It was glad news when we learnt at the end of 1917 that we were now to be treated as an Army and not used piece-meal as divisions and brigades, as we had been in the past at the order of the Army Commander to whom we happened to be attached at the time. This new arrangement was some-thing that we had long wanted and that our leaders had striven for.

The Canadians had insisted on staying together as an Army Corps and were never split up—why not the Aus-tralians? But our divisions and brigades had been treated as 'gap-fillers' to be pushed here and there when other divisions failed to reach their objectives or were in a tight spot. Notwithstanding the efforts of the Australian Government and Mr W. M. Hughes, the War Office would not consent, nor would the British Government intervene, to have this brought about. Now, however, Australians were entirely under their own divisional commanders. One reason might have been that up to this time Australian senior officers were not considered experienced enough, or were not available.

We were sorry to see go such outstanding and brilliant officers as the Englishmen, Major-General 'Hookie' Walker commanding the 1st Division, Sir Neville Smyth, V.C., com-manding the 2nd Division, and Sir H. V. Cox and Brigadier-Generals Leslie and Skene, who were transferred to make room for Australian commanders. In deference to his long association as G.O.C. of the A.I.F., General Birdwood re-tained this post until the end of the war, although the position was held more or less in name only, Monash being the real Commander with Brigadier-General Blamey as his Chief of Staff.

After Monash received his promotion to Lieutenant-General the first thing he did was to prepare a plan to straighten the Line opposite Amiens by attacking and capturing a village called Hamel. There had been no serious British offensive since the Passchendaele operations in 1917 and at first Monash had great difficulty in getting permission to go ahead with his plan; but eventually the High Command consented to it.

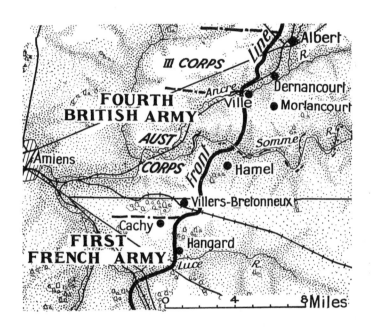

The Amiens Front, 1 May 1918: the dangerous front line that needed straightening opposite Hamel, from Villers-Bretonneux northwards, which gave observation by the Germans along the whole Australian Corps front.

In July we of the 1st Division were visited by an Intelligence Officer of the Australian Corps, who brought us up-to-date with an account of the Battle of Hamel. He told us of General Monash's great achievement and how Monsieur

Clemenceau had visited him and, on behalf of France, thanked him for saving Amiens. He told how Monash had several reasons to carry out this attack. First and foremost, he said, too many English commanders kept looking over their shoulders to see how far away the coast was, and he wanted a victory to help morale—particularly as the Line needed straightening throughout the length of his Corps front; the capture of Hamel would not only deny enemy observation but would improve our jumping-off positions in the event of future operations. He also wanted to test out a new plan for the better employment of tanks. Australian troops had no confidence in tanks. We had been let down badly by them at Bullecourt twelve months previously and our men had suffered heavily in casualties as a consequence. The word 'tank' was anathema to us. However, a new tank had been built that gave promise though it had not yet been used in battle. The men of the Tank Corps had had special training and were very keen. They had some brilliant officers and were on their mettle to show what they could do, but the big job was to restore to Australians their lost confidence in the tank and the Tank Corps. This problem was overcome by taking the Australian Brigade that was to take part in the contemplated operation to a village in a back area, where the men were billeted with members of the Tank Corps. Here they were taken for joyrides and allowed to explore the tanks, inside and out. They thus made pals of the tank crews and became firm friends.

The new method of attack was to treat the tanks as an infantry weapon and advance level with the infantry.

The American 33rd Division had been training with our 4th Division and Monash got approval from Haig for eight of their companies to be distributed through the two Australian brigades that were to take part in the attack, but at the last moment General Pershing refused permission to use them as he was against allowing his men to be split up. Eventually, only one thousand Americans took part and that was only after Monash insisted. Otherwise he would have had to call the attack off as plans could not be altered at that late hour. This was the first occasion in the war when American troops fought in an offensive battle in France: 4 July 1918.

Although only eight Australian battalions were used in the attack, the area attacked was four times greater than in the usual British attacks of 1917, where men were packed tight on a narrow front and in depth. After the battle it was reported that no previous engagement passed off so smoothly or was so free of any kind of hitch. It was all over in ninety minutes. It attained all its objectives and was a huge success.

Congratulations rolled in to General Monash from all the Empire, from the British Prime Minister and the Prime Ministers of Canada, New Zealand and Newfoundland. The Commonwealth Government sent the following message:

> Congratulations on brilliant success of battle . . . achievement will have most considerable military and political effect upon Allies and neutrals and will heighten *moral* of all Imperial Forces.*

Monsieur Clemenceau, Prime Minister of France, as well as Lloyd George, Prime Minister of England, made special visits to Australian Corps Headquarters for the purpose of thanking the troops. Monsieur Clemenceau in the course of his address used these words:

> . . . French people . . . expected a great deal of you, because they have heard what you have accomplished in the development of your own country . . . We knew you would fight a real fight but we did not know that from the very

* Monash, p. 61.

beginning you would astonish the whole Continent with your valour ... I shall go back tomorrow and say to my countrymen: 'I have seen the Australians; I have looked into their eyes. I know that they, men who have fought great battles in the cause of freedom, will fight on alongside us, till the freedom for which we are all fighting is guaranteed for us and our children.*

This was the first offensive operation of any size that had been fought in France since the previous autumn and the effect was electric. It marked the termination of the purely defensive attitude of the British Command.

Shortly after the battle British General Headquarters paid General Monash the compliment of publishing to the whole British Army a Staff Brochure containing the complete Orders in detail and the battle plans, with an official commentary upon them stating at the end: 'Last but most important of all was the skill, determination and fine fighting spirit of the infantry carrying out the attack'.

The brochure said General Monash's battle orders 'would become a model for all similar enterprises throughout the British Army', these orders were compiled and issued by Monash's Chief of Staff, Brigadier-General T. A. Blamey.

We were all thrilled by this report of the magnificent work of our Anzac Corps and longed for the day when we would be moved down to join them, but at the same time we were proud of the fact that the Second Army said they could not spare us from the defence of Hazebrouck.

The 1st Division went on serving with the XV Corps in the Second Army in Flanders altogether for a period of four months. General Monash was reported to have said that he was unable to persuade G.H.Q. to release the Division, such was the importance of its reliability.

---

* *ibid.*, pp. 62-3.

A Triumph of Individual Effort

Diary continues: 10th July 1918

When we dug our trenches on the edge of the Nieppe Forest on April 13th the whole of the ground to our front was a cultivated field. After we had been there a few weeks a wheat crop grew up and was soon waist high. A few men of the 5th Battalion crawled out through the high wheat crop that now covered the ground in front of their posts and suddenly jumping into an enemy post whilst the Huns were half asleep, captured the lot and brought them in. This started what became known as 'Peaceful Penetration.'

The next day's Intelligence Report referred to the incident and the Divisional Intelligence Officer made the laconic statement that it would be interesting to see if the 'peaceful penetration' could be developed throughout the remainder of the Divisional Front. This started a competition amongst the companies in the line to see which company could capture the most prisoners. And so day after day along the whole of the Brigade Front prisoners were captured and brought in.

One day the Huns in front got so scared at this continual penetration that they abandoned their posts and retired back about a mile behind a ridge. The 5th Battalion Platoon Commander responsible for this enemy debacle then went across to the Tommy Battalion on his right flank and told the English Platoon Commander about it and said, 'Come on up and bring your platoon up level with mine.' 'I can't do that!' replied the Englishman, 'you had better get your company commander to see my company commander!'—which he did, but was told, 'I can't do anything about it. You had better get your Colonel to see my Colonel and tell him'—which he also did and the English Colonel said, 'It's a matter for the Brigadier. Get your Brigadier to tell mine.'

That day I happened to be Divisional Liaison Officer—a

daily appointment, a sort of A.D.C. to the General—and I was at Divisional Headquarters and heard the conversation when the English Divisional Commander on our right flank next door strode in about four o'clock in the afternoon. 'Glasgow,' he said, 'what's this I hear that the whole Front opposite your Division is open, the Huns having cleared out and your people are asking mine to advance with them to occupy the ridge opposite?' 'Well,' replied General Glasgow, 'if the platoon and company officers in the front line say so it must be true. After all they are the only ones in a position to know what's going on up there.' 'Well, in that case,' said the English General, 'I will give the order to my people to advance their front too!' and off he went.

But eight hours had gone by since the 5th Battalion Subaltern had asked his opposite number to move up. Shortly afterwards a signal reached Divisional Headquarters to the effect that the Huns had brought up a new Division and were preparing to attack and that with an open flank and in the face of this, the 5th Battalion had no other course open to them but to withdraw to their previously held positions. Two weeks later a planned attack by the 19th Corps, under whom we were now working and attached to, carried out an attack and captured the ridge in question but with the loss of a great many casualties!

How differently the Aussies worked from the Tommies!

27th July 1918

We relieved the 11th Battalion who had carried out a limited attack to straighten the line and had advanced it about 1,000 yards. We found they had not had time to dig a continuous trench but each man had dug a 'funk hole' about waist deep by 3 feet wide and 4 feet long. Our job would be to join all these holes up thus making a continuous trench.

Owing to the shortage of junior officers caused by casualties and the return of several senior company commanders from hospital, I had to revert to the command of a platoon. The relief was complete about midnight. Our platoon front extended for about 300 yards. I looked round to see where to put myself under cover for the coming day and with my batman I walked the length of my platoon front. My batman chose a spot for me but I suddenly had a definite premonition of danger and walked up and down my front several times. Every time I stopped and took up a position in a dugout to rest in I was out again in a few minutes. At last I said to my batman, 'You choose a place for yourself Newman and settle down in it whilst I find somewhere else.' Eventually I decided where to stop and jumped into an unoccupied funk hole and spread myself out to get some sleep, leaving my equipment on except my pack which I used as a pillow. I dozed off to sleep and after daybreak I rose up and looked out to see what my 'front' looked like. The enemy trenches were beyond sight, all was silent in the early morning light when suddenly I heard a German 5.9 gun fire in the distance nearly two miles away—sound travelling faster than the shell—but I could hear the noise of it travelling towards me. This is it I felt, it's going to get me! I knew it would happen, I felt it last night clearly and distinctly. The shell 'had my name on it' as the diggers used to say and believe. As the sound of the shell approached I bent low down in the funk hole—the shell burst, not on top of me but about a yard in front, burying itself beneath me before exploding. I was buried up to my neck. My men rushed and dug me out, amazed that I was still alive. Parts of my equipment were blown off me and as some of my men said, 'We saw your pack blown high in the air and thought it must be part of your body and remarked, there's old "Joynty" gone.' A piece of the shell was resting against one of my knees and burnt my fingers when I removed it as it was red hot. I vomited continuously for some time afterwards, but would not allow myself to be treated as a casualty. I carried on for the remainder of the tour until we were relieved a week later, I felt very sick but still able to remain on duty—fortunately the front remained calm.

That was the only shot fired at us by the Germans that day —a single shot from a 5.9 battery!

Back to the Somme and our own Corps

2nd August 1918

Hurrah! The news that we are to move down to the Somme area to join our Anzac Corps has caused great excitement. The move is to be carried out secretly, mostly at night. Our 1st Brigade has already preceded us.

We handed over our sector to the re-formed 29th Division and at night entrained at Strazeele travelling all night and detraining at a secret railway siding near Amiens at dawn next morning. Before we entrained a special communication was received from the 2nd Army Commander expressing his appreciation of the work done by our Division during its tour in the Hazebrouck and Strazeele area and saying how all ranks of the Army were sorry to lose us. Also, the Corps Commander XV Corps, Lieutenant-General de Lisle sent a letter which we read to our men, couched in the most enthusiastic language, how we had defeated nine German Divisions whilst we were in his Corps.

I kept my Company copy—the letter put our fellows in great heart to know our work was so appreciated.

6th/7th August 1918

After a tiring nine miles route march through the night from our detraining siding near Amiens, we bivouacked at Corbie in the morning. We marched in full 'marching order' full packs, overcoats, rolled blanket and two days rations. We were so fit that practically no men fell out.

It was obvious a big offensive was about to take place. All the roads leading forward were crammed with movement, troops, tanks, artillery—we realised later, all endeavouring to get into position before dawn. Aeroplanes were flying overhead and we were told afterwards this was to drown the noise of the moving transport and tanks. We lay 'doggo' all next day in the cover of the village waiting for orders. In the afternoon after we had rested, Lieutenant-General Monash's Special Order of the Day was read to the troops.

Postscript: Lieut-General Sir John Monash's Special Order of the Day

I kept the copy I had been issued with sensing that it would be a document of tremendous historical value. Every word he wrote came true. Here it is:

Corps Headquarters
August 7th, 1918

To the Soldiers of The Australian Army Corps

For the first time in the history of this Corps, all five Australian Divisions will tomorrow engage in the largest and most important battle operation ever undertaken by the Corps.

They will be supported by an exceptionally powerful Artillery, and by Tanks and Aeroplanes on a scale never previously attempted. The full resources of our sister Dominion, the Canadian Corps, will also operate on our right, while two British Divisions will guard our left flank.

The many successful offensives which the Brigades and Battalions of this Corps have so brilliantly executed during the past four months have been but a prelude to, and the preparation for, this greatest and culminating effort.

Because of the completeness of our plans and dispositions, of the magnitude of the operations, of the number of troops employed, and of the depth to which we intend to over-run the enemy's positions, this battle will be one of the most memorable of the whole war; we shall inflict blows upon the enemy which will make him stagger, which will bring the end appreciably nearer.

I entertain no sort of doubt that every Australian soldier will worthily rise to so great an occasion, and that every man, imbued with the spirit of victory, will, in spite of every difficulty that may confront him, be animated by no other resolve than grim determination to see through to a clean finish, whatever his task may be.

The work to be done tomorrow will perhaps make heavy demands upon the endurance and staying powers of many of you; but I am confident that, in spite of excitement, fatigue, and physical strain, every man will carry on to the utmost of his powers until his goal is won; for the sake of AUSTRALIA, the Empire and our cause.

I earnestly wish every soldier of the Corps the best of good fortune, and a glorious and decisive victory, the story of which will re-echo throughout the world, and will live for ever in the history of our home land.

JOHN MONASH,
Lieut.-General,
Cmdg. Australian Corps.

The Eve of The Great Attack leading to Germany's Black Day

Diary continues: 7th August 1918

After the reading of this message of the Corps Commander to the troops all were thrilled, morale was never so high, in spite of the weakened strength of the battalions due to lack of reinforcements. We were impatient for the offensive to start.

When the list of those detailed to remain in the 'Nucleus' was received, to my horror my name was included. What a shock! To miss this great event was a terrible blow to me. I immediately went to the Adjutant, Capt. Wallis M.C. and asked to be 'paraded' to the Colonel. He took me in to him saying, 'Here's Joynt, Sir, he's terribly upset at being left out and wants to go in, says he has never been left out of any engagement yet since he joined the Battalion.' 'No Joynt,' the Colonel replied, 'you are not fit. I heard all about you being blown up and buried last week. You have got to rest.' 'Well Sir, will you send for me to fill the first replacement necessary?' 'Yes, I will do that,' he grinned. So half a loaf is better than no bread I thought as I returned to my billet, I would get my chance later.

At a conference of officers in the evening the C.O. explained that the plan provided for an attack on a two Division front supported by two Divisions, the Canadians on the right using the same formation whilst the 1st Australian Division and the British Cavalry, supported by Armoured Cars were to be in Close Reserve ready to exploit a break through.

Our 5th Division on the left, occupying the ground that the 3rd British Corps were to take over, had carried out an attack a few days previously to straighten the line on that front and were then relieved by the Tommies so that three Corps were now in line. The Canadians on the right, the Australian Corps in the centre and the British 3rd Corps on the left.

Hardly had this manoeuvre taken place when the Germans attacked and seized the ground won by our 5th Division but now held by the 3rd Corps, capturing 8 officers and 274 other ranks. This German success caused a lot of confusion, coming as it did on the eve of the great attack to be commenced in three days. Members of our 5th Division were very bitter at the failure of the English troops to be in a position to protect their flank when the offensive started. It now meant that the Germans would be able to enfilade them.

Besides that, it was feared that the English prisoners, under interrogation by the Germans, might give away information of the forthcoming offensive.

Postscript: a defence

But this was not so. Captured German officers later were full of praise for the English soldiers' steadfast loyalty under examination. They refused to talk or give any sign of the impending British attack. This suggests that it was not weakness on the part of the Tommies that made them surrender the territory handed over to them by the 5th Division, it was more likely bad leadership. When I was told about this happening, Lord Wolsley's famous saying came to my mind: 'In the British Army there are no bad soldiers only bad officers'.

Germany's Black Day

Diary continues: 8th August 1918

The beginning of our united offensive dawned with a heavy fog covering the landscape and visibility down to about 20 yards. Our artillery barrage opened at 4.20 with a thunderous roar, over a thousand guns opened fire. We in the nucleus were all out on the road bemoaning the fact that we were not taking part in this gigantic battle that would open the way to the winning of the war and bring glory to Australia.

Quite soon we knew things were going well as groups of German prisoners under escort passed us by on the way to the 'prison cage'. Gradually the number increased, first a few bunches then in hundreds and later, in thousands. What a victory was being won!

Occasionally messages reached our O.C. Nucleus, Major Traill to the effect that 'everything was going well, our attack a complete surprise to the enemy, their artillery over-run and now ceased firing, first objectives captured with many guns and provisions.' Another message stated 'Huns taken by surprise, offering no resistance, are surrendering wholesale.'

At mid-day a message that caused us all a tremendous delight was that General Hobb's Division had captured all its objectives and the Australian Flag hoisted at Harbonnieres and the further information that a request was being made to Australian Headquarters in London that this message be sent to the Governor-General of Australia on behalf of the Australian Corps.

In the late afternoon a message arrived that a whole German Corps Headquarters was captured and at nine o'clock we learnt that our attack had exceeded all expectations, our own Corps captures exceeding a total of 8,000 prisoners and 100 guns—some heavy and railway guns and hundreds of vehicles and Regimental transports—and our own casualties for the whole of our Corps would not exceed 1,200.

There was also a message that the Canadians had done well too and captured thousands of prisoners.

We hardly got any sleep that night. We were so interested in learning direct from officers returning from the front personal stories of the overwhelming victory gained that day, and stories of the gallantry and dash of the English Armoured Car Regiment consisting of 16 cars, who penetrated in front of our infantry after objectives were captured, going over ten miles into German territory, blowing up bridges and capturing German Generals in their Headquarters. The surprise was so great at the sudden appearance in their Headquarters of armed car crews that they offered no resistance. We were told our Diggers couldn't speak too highly of their dash and bravery.

There was one blemish though to the day's success, told by an officer of our 4th Division, and that was the failure of the English 3rd Corps on their left to keep up and win their objective for the day with the result that the enemy remained in possession of the heights overlooking their left flank. The German artillery situated there was able to fire point blank at the nine tanks allotted to the 4th Division and put them out of action one by one. Besides this, instead of our left Brigade pushing on, it had to fight sideways.

In the official Corps Intelligence report next day we read that 'the enemy on the front of the 3rd Corps had resisted strongly,' that 'fighting had been fierce and no progress could be made.'

10th August 1918

News has reached us that the 8th Battalion is fighting on the extreme right flank and this was the scene of very severe fighting following the advance of the 1st Australian Division the night before to the foot of the Lihons Ridge.

11th August 1918

The advance is continuing in sympathy with the 2nd Division and the Canadian Corps.

The enemy fought hard and determinedly to retain Lihons Knoll and made many counter-attacks but they were successfully driven off by rifle and machine gun fire without us losing any ground. 'This advance, and the holding of the ground won, was a great feat by the 1st Division and ranks among the best performances of any troops during the war' —so ran the daily intelligence report. Some 20 field guns and hundreds of machine guns were captured.

Postscript: a comment from Monash

In his report of this action by the 1st Australian Division General Monash wrote: 'Such a battle ... would, in 1917, have been placarded as a victory of the first magnitude. Now with the new standards set by the great battle of August 8th, it was reckoned merely as a local skirmish.'*

Diary continues: 13th August 1918

We in the Nucleus, hearing that our Battalion was now in Reserve, prompted McGinn and myself with the desire to go up and see them so we begged Major Traill the O.C. to concoct a message as an excuse for us both to take up to the Colonel and so see our comrades and learn all about their wonderful work, and also to see the area of the country won from the enemy.

We set off in the morning and hitch-hiked our way by jumping on to motor transport trucks carrying material up to the front line, and then tracking down to where the 8th Battalion was resting. It was indeed an experience to see the result of the great victory in the amount of booty won and German prisoners in their hundreds, slowly making their way to the rear some with, but many without escorts. Never before had there been such a scene on the Western Front as we travelled mile after mile for 13 miles. We were hardly able to contain ourselves, so great was our excitement.

We had lunch with Battalion Headquarters staff and bit by bit were told the outstanding incidents of the three days fighting.

The Colonel told us what a terrific time the Battalion had had after marching from Corbie some of the night and most of the day carrying full equipment—rolled blanket, overcoat and three days rations—a distance of 13 miles on a very hot day then, without proper reconnaissance, at 4.30 in the afternoon were thrown into an attack advancing across open country. This without proper artillery support or tanks, against heavily defended German positions with concealed machine gun posts. They had been given a terrific task but

* Monash, p. 140.

they did it! But our casualties were tremendously heavy, over one-third of the Battalion becoming casualties.

He was loud in the praise of the fighting spirit of the troops and their gallantry, particularly the extraordinary bravery of Private Beatham who, when the advance was held up by heavy machine gun fire dashed forward and with only one man with him (Lance Corporal Nottingham M.M.), bombed and fought the crews of four enemy machine guns killing ten of them and capturing ten others. Later in the attack he again dashed forward and bombed a machine gun but in doing so was killed, his body being riddled with bullets. He was being recommended for a posthumous Victoria Cross and, as the Colonel said, 'was that Decoration ever better earned?' The men were all talking about his exploit and coming forward to give their evidence. The Colonel added, 'bravery alone is not sufficient to win a Victoria Cross, it needs valour of a kind that, by its action, leads to a strategical victory of importance, and that is just what the loss to the Germans of those machine guns did, the consequent drop in enemy fire power enabled the Battalion to move forward and win the final objective.*

Colonel Mitchell was also full of praise for our O.C. 'D' Company, Captain Campbell, for the way he handled the Company. On his own initiative Campbell manoeuvred his men round to the rear of a strongly defended copse and attacked the Huns from the rear capturing the position with some hundreds of Germans (for this he was recommended and won the D.S.O.), but later he was wounded and when carried into the R.A.P. the Medical Officer said to him, 'Well, where have they wounded you this time. "Wear Wanks"?' 'Same place,' replied Campbell. The doctor then knew where to look and turned him over and sure enough, saw the wound where he expected. Twice previously Alec had been wounded

---

* Beatham was awarded the V.C. posthumously.

in the buttocks by shrapnel (not bullets) and this was the third time in practically the same place! His nickname 'Wear Wanks' was given to him shortly after the Battalion arrived in France and Campbell was made Battalion Bombing Officer. Being of Scottish descent, Alec couldn't pronounce his R's, and on the occasion of taking over his Bombing Section he fell them in and inspected them and then addressing them said, 'the fwont wanks all wight but the wear wanks wotten.' (The nickname 'Wear Wanks' stuck to him for the whole of the war, and afterwards too.)

The Colonel continued, there was no co-ordination with the Canadian Corps on our right and we were without proper artillery or tank support. The three days fighting that followed was the severest and heaviest that the Battalion had experienced in the whole of its history.

Whereas the Canadians always attacked at dawn when the mist covered the ground, our troops through delayed planning, were not positioned to attack on this occasion until later in the morning when the sun had dispersed the mist and they then had to face strongly defended localities, heavy machine gun and rifle fire from concealed enemy positions.

Our casualties were tremendously heavy in consequence. Who was to blame for it all, he did not know—but one thing was certain—instead of 4th Army (Rawlinson) directing the plan, Zero hour for each attack was determined by the Canadian Corps at times when it was impossible for the Australians to conform.

Postscript: the critics

Severe criticism of this action of the Ist Australian Division was commonplace: 'How not to exploit a successful attack.' 'The attack in daylight, across the open fields should never have been made!' 'Something went wrong—who was to blame? Was it the Canadian's timing at fault?' 'It seemed another "Charge of the Light Brigade" fiasco—except in this case all objectives were gained and a great victory won, but at what unnecessary cost!'

Diary continues

The Colonel said the 2nd and 3rd Brigade's casualty list, with the exception of Pozières, was the heaviest-ever suffered in local attacks—100 officers fell and 1,500 other ranks. Notwithstanding this lack of proper co-ordination the spirit of the men had never been so high. On one occasion, realising the futility of continuing the attack across open ground against a continuous hail of machine gun bullets he ordered the Battalion to stop and seek cover in the shelter of the folding ground. The 6th Battalion then charged over them, their officers shouting, 'if the 8th can't do it the 6th will.' It was brave but foolish and the 6th soon saw that it was so and went to ground and stayed under cover same as the 8th, virtually licking their wounds.

He went on to say the Battalion later had fought two big battles as part of the Division and then a third one on their own. The Germans were still in possession of a commanding ridge about 2,000 yards long and it so happened that he picked up the field telephone that had just been laid to talk to Brigade Headquarters and overheard a conversation between the Brigadier and one of the other Battalion Commanders in which the Brigadier had just ordered that Battalion to carry out an attack on the ridge but the Battalion Commander was demurring, saying his men were so done and their casualties so heavy that they were no longer capable of effective action. Colonel Mitchell remained silent whilst he listened and mentally considered the situation and the possibilities of a successful operation being carried out. He then heard the Brigadier say, 'Well, if you can't do it I will ask the 8th Battalion.' Colonel Mitchell put the phone down and waited. Shortly it rang and the Brigadier spoke,

'Mitchell,' he said, 'I want you to attack and capture that Hill—can you do it?' 'Yes I can,' replied the Colonel, 'if you will allow me to make my own dispositions and the time of assault.' 'Granted,' replied the Brigadier. The C.O. explained to me he knew the usual time for the Germans to dismantle and clean their machine guns was just before dark. He decided to attack on a wide front and spread the men along it a man to every 20 yards and then, without any artillery support and in the quietness of the early evening the men were told to charge and shout at the top of their voices. The Germans, on hearing the loud shouting no doubt thought it was a superior force attacking. It was too much for them, they leapt up and ran from the line they were holding. Our Diggers chased them over the hill and then dug in. The easiest stunt ever carried out by the Battalion—a major enemy position captured with only a loss of twenty casualties. Once again the Germans showed they were no good at hand-to-hand fighting and when it came to close quarters also surrendered or fled.

Our presence at the Battalion without being sent for came in for some pretended adverse criticism by the Colonel. 'How is it,' he asked, 'that two senior Company officers arrive here with a message no more important than the equivalent of wanting to know if the Battalion is running out of cocoa? If they had said Rum there might have been a justifiable reason for their "escapade"!' Anyhow, he didn't pursue the subject and told us to return to the nucleus as the Battalion was being relieved and was coming out to rest next day.

On the way back to the Nucleus Camp we saw Canadian troops having done their job, withdrawing. Evidently they were being returned to their own familiar hunting ground, the Vimy Ridge area opposite Arras. No doubt to again be the spearhead in a future offensive on that front. A kilted Division, the 32nd Scottish were moving up to replace them.

On the first day's fighting (August 8th) the Canadians had

taken over 5,000 prisoners at a cost of 1,038 killed. Our Australian Corps had sent back about 8,000 prisoners out of a total haul from the three Corps of 19,000. Our Corps losses were only a mere 652 casualties with only 83 killed. Surely the cheapest victory ever gained in any war and a tribute to our Corps Commander's tactics and planning. The English 3rd Corps collected 3,000 prisoners but the 'follow through' tactics were a tragedy and an example of how NOT to exploit a successful attack. Our 1st Division losses alone being twice as great as the losses of the whole Anzac Corps on August 8th.

We learnt with pleasure that General Monash, two days previously, was Knighted, the King having arrived at Corps Headquarters and in the presence of 500 picked Australian troops—100 from each of our five Divisions—the King had drawn his sword and 'dubbed' our admired and respected Corps Commander. A Knighthood granted in the Field—in the presence of the men he commanded—in like manner and in the same tradition that Queen Elizabeth the First had Knighted Sir Francis Drake on the quarterdeck of the 'Golden Hind.'

Postscript: the German point of view

The German General Ludendorff said in his *Memoirs*, reprinted in *The Times,* 22 August 1919:

> August 8th was the black day of the German Army in the history of the war. This was the worst experience I had to go through . . . Early on August 8th, in a dense fog that had been rendered still thicker by artificial means, the British, mainly with Australian and Canadian Divisions, and French, attacked between Albert and Moreuil with strong squadrons of Tanks, but for the rest with no great superiority. They broke between the Somme and the Luce deep into our front. The Divisions in line allowed themselves to be completely overwhelmed. Divisional Staffs

were surprised in the Headquarters by enemy Tanks [*sic*, our armoured cars were meant]... The exhausted (*sic*) Divisions that had been relieved a few days earlier and that were lying in the region south-west of Peronne were immediately alarmed and set in motion by the Commander-in-Chief of the Second Army. At the same time he brought forward towards the breach all available troops. The Rupprecht Army Group dispatched reserves thither by train. The 18th Army threw its own reserves directly into the battle from the south-east... On an order from me, the 9th Army too, although itself in danger, had to contribute. Days of course elapsed before the troops from a further distance could reach the spot... It was a very gloomy situation... Six or seven Divisions that were quite fairly to be described as effective had been completely battered... The situation was uncommonly serious. If they continued to attack with even comparative vigour, we should no longer be able to maintain ourselves west of the Somme... The wastage of the Second Army had been very great. Heavy toll had also been taken of the reserves which had been thrown in... Owing to the deficit created our losses had reached such proportions that the Supreme Command was faced with the necessity of having to disband a series of Divisions, in order to furnish drafts... The enemy had also captured documentary material of inestimable value to him... The General Staff Officer whom I had dispatched to the battlefield on August 8th, gave me such an account that I was deeply confounded... August 8th made things clear for both Army commands, both for the German and for that of the enemy.*

Sir John Monash, after quoting Ludendorff's comments, wrote regarding the 8 August offensive by his corps:

The tactical value of the victory was immense, and has never yet been fully appreciated by the public of the Empire, perhaps because our censorship at the time strove to conceal the intention to follow it up immediately

* Monash, p. 130.

with further attacks. But no better testimony is needed than that of Ludendorff himself, who calls it Germany's 'black day', after which he himself gave up all hope of a German victory.*

The Anzac Corps by this time, with its attached troops—the Cavalry Corps, the Tank Battalions and two attached British Divisions plus Labour Corps—numbered more men than any of the other armies in France. Well over 200,000 men in all, but General Haig still would not consent to the Corps being called an Army and given the prestige of what that would mean to the Corps senior officers.

Diary continues: 16th August 1918

The nucleus personnel rejoined the Battalion where they were bivouacked on the banks of the River Somme, a delightful area that had never been fought over and here we rested, doing nothing in the way of drill or exercises. The weather was perfect, we swam in the river and sunbathed on the banks.

The strength of the Battalion was sadly depleted, 12 officer casualties and 224 O/ranks were lost in the previous week's fighting. Usually we would have been built up to strength by a draft of reinforcements both from the convalescent camps in England and new drafts from Australia, but the depots were all empty. Recruiting had practically stopped in Australia so we were told, notwithstanding General Monash's appeal for men to come forward.

The Australian Prime Minister, Mr W. M. Hughes had attempted to bring in Conscription to build up the A.I.F. There was a referendum which was heavily defeated. Members of the A.I.F. in a majority voted against it. According to the men of my own platoon their attitude was—if men won't come voluntarily we don't want them. Also, disloyal

* *ibid.*

Irish led by Dr. Mannix, the Roman Catholic Archbishop of Melbourne, and the left wing of the Labour Party, strongly fought against it.

At a second attempt by the Australian Government the referendum figures showed a remarkable change of attitude by the people generally, and by the A.I.F. who this time gave a majority in favour. However, the referendum was again defeated although by only a small majority.

Notwithstanding this lack of support from Australia the morale of the 'diggers' continued high. Never before in the war were such stories told of the extraordinary deeds of individual gallantry as those that were going the rounds of the troops. Some of the stories told were almost unbelievable in their daring and initiative, particularly in the way isolated bodies of Australians and in some cases, individual diggers, crossed over to the British 3rd Corps' Sector and joined in with the Tommies who seemed to have no idea of how to overcome German machine gun posts.

For instance, when the English 3rd Corps failed to make progress opposite Chipilly on our left flank two Sappers of the 12th Australian Field Coy., working on repairing a bridge, observed from their point of vantage in rear of the 4th Australian Division that the English flank company was held up by a nest of machine gunners on a forward ridge so they decided, on their own accord, to end the impasse themselves by rushing the enemy position from the flank. They ran across an open field several hundred yards wide and attacked the German machine gunners from their rear. The Germans, apparently thinking they were part of a large force, hoisted a white flag. The 'Londons' then came forward and carried on to the next spur.

Another most fantastic story, told with enthusiasm by observers of the incident, was how a patrol of four men under two senior N.C.O's. of the 1st Battalion (Australian) crossed the river and spoke to the Company Commander of a London battalion whose men were sheltering under cover, obviously reluctant to advance towards the village of Chipilly their objective, which was on the left of the 1st Australian Brigade, outflanking the Australian advance south of the village and from where serious enfilading fire was hampering the Australian advance on that sector. To the suggestion of the two N.C.O's. to follow the patrol who would lead the way, the London Company Commander turned a deaf ear. The Australians then said they 'would go it alone.' The English Company Commander endeavoured to dissuade them but spreading themselves out with intervals of twelve yards between each man, they charged forward—the enemy opened fire but the wide front (about sixty yards) enabled the patrol to reach the village unhurt. They surrounded and captured a German post and took thirty prisoners. The Tommies then came up and these prisoners were handed over to them. Then showing the Londons how to attack defended localities, the diggers led the Tommies by a succession of rushes and captured post after post of Germans finally capturing the spur from which the Germans were hampering the 1st Brigade's advance; altogether handing over 200 prisoners, they then returned to their own lines but carrying with them a signed letter from the English Company Commander addressed to their C.O., giving an appreciation of what they had done and extolling their bravery and leadership.

Postscript: the capture of Chipilly

The following is Bean's account of the Capture of Chipilly.

> . . . a Company of the 2nd/10th London [Battalion] next to the Somme could be seen still sheltering half a mile from Chipilly.
>
> At 5.50 p.m. Brig-Genl. Mackay of the Ist Brigade ordered Major Mackenzie of the Ist Battalion to send across the

river a patrol under a couple of N.C.O.'s who had been through Chipilly village earler that morning, searching for souvenirs and had urged that they should be allowed to take out a patrol. [The two diggers had gone out, unarmed, across the bridge and not being shot at, had entered Chipilly. There they picked up two German rifles and stalked a chalk pit north of the village. It was empty except for a machine gun which they brought back. Hearing shouts in English as they returned they had walked to a British post half a mile west and after learning its news of the Tommies 'hold up' returned with the information to their Company Commander.] As the British were about to attack, the request had been refused; but now the two—Coy. Q.M. Sgt. Hayes and his friend Sgt. Andrews were told to take four men, find out what was stopping the attack and, if possible, help it forward.

Crossing at 6 p.m. Hayes went first to the company of the 2/10 London. Its Commander, Capt. Berrell, advised them not to go but the village was enticing and after extending to 12 paces interval, the six Australians made the rush and, though heavily fired at from the ridge north of the village, got through unscathed. Berrell now brought up half his company which, as it reached them, was fired on by a machine-gun in the valley to the north, losing some men. Meanwhile the Australians, after searching the village in two parts, worked up the spur northward and here sighted a post of Germans all intent upon their front. Ptes. Stevens and Turpin were left to guard the village entrance. Pte. Kane, a runner, was sent to the 2/10th Londons to guide up a Lewis gun crew. Andrews and Pte. Fuller pushed round to the back of Chipilly spur and Hayes, after watching two German machine-guns firing in the valley, led a platoon of the English to a chalk pit on the northern outskirts. The obvious course was to take the Germans in flank, but as the platoon arrived the British guns laid a heavy barrage of smoke on this ground. The shells fell close and the platoon was ordered back.

The smoke, however, gave the Australians their chance. Sergt. Andrews and Fuller, who had returned, took Hayes along their previous track more than half a mile around the reverse side of the spur, and there sighted, on the slope above the river, a small German post. While Andrews and Fuller covered it with their fire, Hayes worked round its flank. As he rose to rush it he found himself looking into another post of three men, one of whom fired singeing Hayes' tunic, but missed, and was at once shot by him. The others bolted but on Andrews and Turpin running out firing, they too were captured and rushed back to the chalk pit. Telling the Londons to follow close, Hayes, with Andrews, Fuller and Kane returned under cover of the smoke to the post previously attacked. The Germans in the second post retired, but following them, Andrews and Kane in front, and Hayes and Fuller in flank, sighted a stronger post and bore in upon it, shooting from the hip. The Germans dived into their dugouts from which, in response to a bomb, an officer and 31 men came out. Handing the prisoners to the Londons, who were now coming up, Kane and Fuller went on and captured nine more prisoners and two machine guns. Germans from Chipilly Ridge were now retiring eastward across the Somme. Andrews set up a German machine gun and fired at them ... the Londons came up and the Germans finally broke from the ridge above. With Andrews firing his machine gun, Fuller and Kane took another thirty prisoners. By 10 p.m., having led the British advance the whole way, the patrol returned to its Company. [At 9.15 Cpt. Berrell gave them a note recommending them for their 'conspicuous work and magnificent bravery with me today'. (No mention, however, was made of them in the records of the 2/10th London, an omission which was the real cause of a subsequent newspaper controversy.)]

... Monash, who had a plan for forcing this [part of the 3rd Corps sector] line in conjunction with an advance south of the river, had now persuaded Rawlinson to hand the sector over to him. Rawlinson apparently felt that he could arrange this the more easily as Lieut.-General But ler (III Corps) was going on sick-leave arranged several days before; his position was temporarily taken by Lieut.- General Godley.*

---

* Bean, *Official History...*, vol. vi, pp. 650-3.

Diary continues: 21st August 1918

Our Battalion's period of rest did not last long. After only four days the order came to move up to the line again. The only officer reinforcements we received were two fairly senior officers who had been seconded to the 2nd Brigade training Battalion in England and who, consequently, had missed the heavy fighting in 1917–18—Capt. G. E. Johnston and Lieut. C. Findlay. The Battalion had never been so weak in officers, N.C.O's. and men. Platoons were down to only 15 to 20 men. Nevertheless, the spirit of the men was extraordinarily high. We route marched all day and half the night, arriving at a line of dugouts and trenches near Proyart at midnight. The night was clear with a brilliant moon showing. The men stood the long march well, singing and whistling most of the time. The cookers had preceded the column and a hot drink was served to the men on arriving. Notwithstanding the terrific casualties the Battalion had suffered barely a week previously, the men showed no lack of fighting spirit.

22nd August 1918

In the morning, parties from each of the Companies were sent forward to view the 'forming up area' where we were to attack from next day. Upon the C.O's. return from Brigade Headquarters a conference of company commanders was called and the battle instructions issued. We were also shown the exact position on the actual ground we were to attack over. The shortage of officers meant that I had to revert to the command of a platoon, as Lieut. Findlay, who had returned to the battalion after service in England, was appointed to 'D' Company. He was so very much senior to me being an original 'Anzac' with nearly four year's service, but still only a Lieutenant. I understood the position, it could not be expected for Findlay to serve under me, who was so much his junior in service, I didn't mind a bit. Also, there were so few junior officers still on their feet. As a consequence, platoon sergeants were acting as platoon commanders in all of the companies.

Zero hour for the attack was fixed at 4.45 next morning.

The Battle of Chuignes Valley

23rd August 1918

This attack was to further exploit General Monash's 8th August offensive. It was to be carried out by our 1st Division with the 32nd Scottish Division on our right, and a partly trained American Regiment, attached to the 3rd British Corps (that was not participating) to watch our left flank, but on no account was it to be used as assault troops unless in extreme urgency.

The main objective was the crest of the rising ground beyond the Chuignes Valley, a distance of about 3 miles which gave observation over many miles of country to the east and north. The attack was on a three brigade front.

The 6th and 5th Battalions of the 2nd Brigade were to attack supported by the 8th and 7th Battalions. The 2nd Machine Gun Battalion were in close support to give covering fire.

At midnight we assembled about 1,000 yards behind the outpost line held by the 5th Division. It was a hot night and we laid down in the open. I had become so used to war by this time that I was not at all excited at the prospect of within a few hours being engaged in a heavy battle and as zero hour was not until 4.45 and we were not to move off to the start line until 4 o'clock, I decided to get some sleep and stretched out under the stars after telling my batman to wake me at 4 o'clock. I slept soundly for four hours when my batman woke me and gave me a pannikin of hot cocoa and told me the platoon was 'fallen in' and waiting for me.

We moved off straight away for the start line and as we did so the Germans put down a heavy creeping barrage, about 300 yards deep. Experience of German methods enabled me to get my men safely through the barrage by timing our movements. Knowing that the Germans lifted their range every minute, I used this knowledge to get my men to lie low and wait while I could tell by the sound of the falling shells where they would next strike and in this way I got my men through without a single casualty.

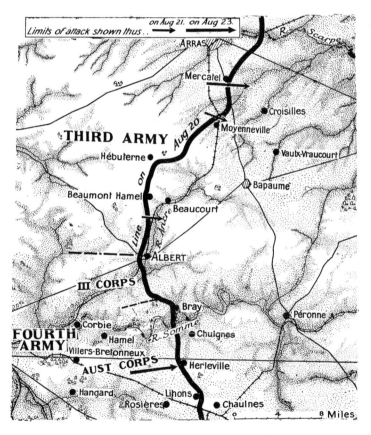

The Battle of Albert, 21-23 August 1918

On reaching our start line I made off to my right and contacted the Company of the Argyle and Sutherland Highlanders of the 32nd Division that was operating on my right flank. We had a yarn about our respective boundaries and then returning to my platoon, got them digging a trench to take cover in if we were shelled. Our support position was about 500 yards behind the attacking troops and we were to remain there until needed or until the 6th captured the final objective another 2,500 yards in front. We would then consolidate our position as a second line of defence.

Just before zero hour, 4.45 the Huns put up a marvellous display of coloured 'very lights'—each colour of course, being a separate sign to the Germans—they must have got wind of our approaching attack! This was followed by a terrific barrage on our front line but as we had moved forward a few hundred yards most of the shells went overhead but our Reserve Companies were badly mauled.

Shortly after the attack started, from a copse on our immediate right a hundred or more German prisoners appeared being shepherded by a dozen or more kilted Highlanders. As they emerged into the open field in front of my platoon front they were observed by German machine gun posts on the distant rise who opened fire on them—a characteristic custom of the Huns to shoot down their own men who had been captured. The poor Huns were in a bad way, they couldn't run back because of the Scotties hunting them forward so they dashed for our trench to get under cover but our own men were sheltering in half-dug holes only a few feet deep, so the Huns couldn't get much cover there, so they ran hither and thither looking for shelter. The kilties were splendid, they never sought cover themselves but kept rounding up the Huns prodding them with bayonets until they got them over the ridge behind us.

Some twenty minutes or so after the attack started I could tell from the sound of the firing the advance had stopped.

Also away on the left, opposite the 5th Battalion front, I could see men retiring—things didn't look too good. I said to my batman, 'let's go and have a look, Newman, and see what's up!' When we had walked about eight hundred yards we found the remnants of a 6th Battalion Company sheltering in a sunken road—all the officers in the Company except one had become casualties, and this one was a new 'reinforcement' officer straight from Australia who had not seen any war service. Heavy machine gun fire was coming from a wood to their left. Poor chap, he was at a loss to know what to do. His was the left company in the attack and was about 600 yards behind the rest of the Battalion. I told him to spread his men out and get them to advance in rushes of twenty-five yards at a time. This they did for a few hundred yards and then they went to earth again.

We watched them from where we stood under cover, meaning to stay where we were but away on the left I could see Germans advancing. It was apparent to me now that there was a wide gap between the 6th and 5th Battalion fronts. 'I think we had better go and ginger them up again, Newman! Things look pretty serious, if the Huns counter-attack through the gap between here and the 5th Battalion, goodness knows what will happen—come on.' The German artillery had shortened their range and now shells instead of flying overhead were falling amongst us. About forty yards away we saw a dead German officer and I said, 'go and rat him,' meaning to search the body for papers. As Newman was bending over the body a shell burst almost on top of him. I rushed to him, blood was gushing from a nasty wound in his throat—a piece of shell had penetrated it—I quickly undid my field bandage and endeavoured to bind the wound but I couldn't tie it tight enough to stop the flow of blood without suffocating him. I could only tie the bandage lightly, using the whole length of bandage. I dragged his body and propped it up against a bank where it could be easily seen. I had to make a decision either to stop with Newman and look after him or press on, as the situation was so serious and leadership was obviously needed in front. I decided to leave Newman and go and take charge of the situation. This I did and soon connected up with the forward company of the 6th Battalion. There I found Lieut. Darby doing a magnificent job—the only surviving officer of the company, he had complete control and was close to his objective but his Company had suffered tremendously.

Enemy fire was coming from a small wood about 300 yards away, between where we were and the 5th Battalion. It seemed to be alive with Germans and machine guns.

Quickly surveying the situation I told Darby I would take the thirty men of the 6th that I had gathered up and send for some of my own men and return to the bottom of the valley and then work my way round to the far side of the small wood and rush it from there. Give me twenty minutes I told him, to get round and in position because it would mean about half a mile to cover altogether, and then get all your men to line the Roman road that we are on and fire like blazes at the wood to keep the Germans with their heads down while we rush it from the other side. And off we went—keeping low and following down the Roman road which was sunken at that part.

At the bottom of the valley road we were halted and had to take cover from a German machine gun that was well posted to cover the intersection of the Roman road and a cross road leading up the valley. We had no Lewis gun and the German gun was in a prepared position, sunk in the ground well protected and concealed from view. Whilst hesitating with my men, holding them under cover of the sunken road and thinking out a plan to attack the post there suddenly appeared Lieut. McGinn and his platoon, running towards us down the valley, shouting out, 'we have got the

Hun—we boxed on with him from up there,' pointing up the valley road.

With McGinn's platoon of twenty men and my thirty, gave me a force of fifty men—just what I wanted to fight my way round and attack Plateau Wood from the other side.

We now crossed the road and there below us in a hollow, saw a number of Germans in a group of huts. We rushed them and captured fifty prisoners. We then found it was an enemy field hospital full of wounded Germans and some of the 5th Battalion men. The two German doctors in charge, to whom I spoke, said, 'Don't treat us as prisoners we will stay here and look after your wounded as well as our own if you will let us.' This I consented to. We sent back under escort several diggers from McGinn's platoon, the fifty prisoners we had captured and then continued on our way. We found an old communication trench leading up the hill towards the top of Plateau Wood and we worked our way up this 'boxing on' with several Hun machine gun posts, capturing more prisoners. We bombed our way eventually to the top where I lined our men along the straight communication trench called Eniscourt Alley, facing the Plateau Wood which was about fifty yards away. The Wood seemed full of Germans. With only fifty men at my disposal it looked too hazardous an operation to charge across the open space that existed in front of us. I refrained from attempting it but the spirit of the diggers was high, they only wanted the order 'Charge' and they would have responded gallantly. Whilst I was deliberating what to do a redheaded digger shouted out, 'Let's rush the b—— place.' 'No,' I shouted back, 'we wouldn't have a chance, there's a line of machine guns facing us. Stand fast all,' I ordered. 'We will find a better way and make sure of it.' The diggers' tails were right up, no need to lead them only to guide them.

I got hold of McGinn and said, 'Come on Mac, let's reconnoitre a bit and see if we can find an old Sap leading into the Wood from the eastern side.' Then to the Senior N.C.O., 'keep the men where they are while we have a look around.' With McGinn's batman and two other diggers as runners we then followed up the old communication trench. It was not occupied. We cautiously crept up it, working our way for a hundred yards or more. Occasionally a Hun scuttled in front of us. We came to an obviously occupied deep dugout. A pile of German hand grenades lay close to its entrance —a digger threw one down the deep stairway, it exploded and we heard shouts. We were all looking at the entrance with our backs turned to the trench when hearing the rattle of accoutrements I turned round to see a party of Huns led by an N.C.O. come around a corner of the trench, right on top of us with their rifles 'at the ready.' A horrible feeling —we are trapped! Only five of us. No escape; the thought— we're prisoners—no, never! The Hun leader had his rifle held at the ready; I was carrying my revolver in my right hand and I acted first. I raised my arm and pointed it at his head. He immediately dropped his rifle and put his hands up. The next German dropped his rifle too and put his hands up and in sequence, as German after German came round the corner, they all did the same. Then several Germans emerged from the dugout crying out 'Merci Kamerad' and they too were holding their hands up. Now there were twenty or more Huns all standing in front of us, their rifles on the ground and their hands up with our three diggers covering them with their fixed bayonets pointed. So far not a word had been spoken and then there emerged, creeping out from the dugout one more Hun, looking scared enough as if he was about to howl, and with his hands held high. McGinn, from his position alongside me took three or four very slow menacing strides towards the cringing Hun and bringing his face close to him said, 'BOO!' The Hun collapsed on his knees and stayed there, hands held high.

The Battle of Chuignes Valley, 23 August 1918: *(above)* Plateau Wood, the objective, and the knoll, as seen from the Start Line of D Coy, 8th Battalion *(below)* St Martins Wood, through which the 5th Battalion attacked on our left but were held up by the Huns' strong defence of Plateau Wood.

The Battle of Chuignes Valley, 23 August 1918: *(above)* Plateau Wood seen from the Roman road, from where Lieut. Darby's Company of the 6th Battalion gave us covering fire while we attacked the wood from the other side; *(below)* the scene of severe fighting on the way to the top of the ridge—the communication trench, now filled in, up which we bombed our way, capturing a field gun and several machine guns and taking about fifty prisoners.

(*Top*). This side of the wood was heavily defended and our few men had to be restrained from attacking it across the open. It was here (*centre*) where a party of Germans surprised us as we were looking down a dugout at the corner of the wood. When covered by my revolver their leader surrendered, followed by the remainder of the Germans. After despatching the prisoners under escort, we continued up another trench we had discovered leading to the wood (*right*).

The capture of Mont St Quentin, 1 September 1918 *(top)* A company of the 21st Battalion left Elsa Trench for the attack. The Australians charged across the open, yelling and shouting *(centre)* and achieved a quick surrender from the bewildered Germans *(bottom).* *Source:* A.W.M.

The three diggers then started 'ratting' the watches from the Huns. I told them—'Hey! You can't do that, its against the rules of war!' 'Well, if we don't take them now others will when the Huns are passed down along the line of communication.' 'Yes, I suppose so. What about a watch for me?' 'Take your pick Sir,' said one of the diggers and coming towards me he held out his clasped hands full of watches. I chose one and put it in my pocket. (Late that day, on taking the watch out of my left tunic pocket I found it smashed by a bullet which had hit the watch and ricocheted off my body. It would have been a nasty wound to my hip and possibly my stomach.)

The situation was now perfectly absurd. Twenty or more Huns all standing with their hands held high, with our diggers 'ratting' them and McGinn and myself looking on with one Hun still on his knees. The reaction was so great that I started to laugh—one minute or second ago all was lost, at best we were prisoners or more likely dead men, and now our lives were safe and we were triumphant. I couldn't stop laughing, it was all so absurd, then McGinn joined in and we just couldn't stop. I suppose it was a sort of hysteria after the strain we had been through. We leaned against the wall of the trench and laughed and laughed—it was some time before we could stop. Then, turning to the Huns I signalled 'get going' and putting two of the diggers as escort, off they went down the trench to the rear, willingly departing. McGinn and I and the other digger continued our way up the trench which led to the top of the copse. We decided this was the place to attack from, good cover and possibly the benefit of a surprise.

We then returned to where our men were. I directed the 6th Battalion men to wait a while before opening fire on to the Wood from where they were whilst Lt. McGinn and his platoon, with myself, would work our way up to the top where we had seen a Sap leading off into the Wood. We would attack from there. The Wood was full of Germans: surprise by attacking from an unexpected direction was our only hope of capturing it. A German machine gun was sweeping the ground to the north and we would attack from the eastern side; this we did. Whilst we were attacking a digger shouted 'they are running' and so they were. We pursued them, shouting. The fire from the 6th Battalion men assisted us. The Germans seemed staggered and to our amazement, we collected in 100 prisoners—an abject surrender—won without the loss of a single casualty.

I went along to the left of our objective which we had now won and told Capt. Permezel of the 5th Battalion that his right flank was secure. I then established three posts on the edge of the copse filling the gap between the 6th and 5th Battalions as the Germans started counter-attacking.

I sent off a message to my Commanding Officer reporting to him what I had done and then looked up Colonel Ulrich, C.O. of the 6th Battalion and informed him of the situation. Unlike Capt. Permezel of the 5th Battalion who greeted me with enthusiasm and relief, Colonel Ulrich was rather cold and formal. I think he felt it that his own Battalion had not fully achieved its objective.

Shortly after this a verbal message reached me from the C.O. that I was to withdraw my men, leaving the 6th Battalion men where they were and return to 'D' Coy. Headquarters. When I got there I found Capt. Johnston, O.C. 'A' Coy. had been killed by the barrage the Huns had sent down when we were forming up before the attack and also Lieut. Findlay, after the attack started.

I automatically took charge of the Coy. and sent off another message to the C.O. explaining more fully what had occurred and that I had assumed command of 'D' Coy. Shortly an order arrived from the C.O. for me to take my Coy. back to the position I had previously occupied between the 5th and 6th Battalions and that I had done well. I was to report to the 6th Battalion when in position but I was to remain under 8th Battalion command and report direct. I did this and established my Coy. Headquarters in the dugout where the cringing Hun had emerged from.

During the morning the Huns started shelling our whole front line and my Coy. suffered several casualties from shell fire. In the early afternoon a Hun counter-attack developed which we easily beat off. We spent the rest of the day in consolidating our position. The German gunfire remained constant and our casualties began to mount.

24th August 1918

We 'stood to' all the night manning our posts to be ready if the Hun again counter-attacked in force but dawn came much to our relief with everything quiet on our particular front. Leaving McGinn in charge of the Coy. I took the opportunity to get some rest. The dugout I occupied as my Headquarters was well fitted up with several good bunks, evidently it had been a Headquarters. I selected a comfortable bunk and laid down, sleeping for several hours. After I awoke my A/Sgt Major informed me that the C.O. had called but would not allow him to wake me. He had come to have a look round and expressed himself as very pleased with the work of the Coy. and the way we had consolidated our position. The rest of the day passed quietly. From our position on the knoll we could see plenty of action amongst the Germans away on our right opposite the Scotties.

At 10 p.m. that night another two companies of the 8th Battalion came into the line and the 8th Battalion took over from the 6th Battalion with our four companies in line with the 6th Battalion in support.

At 8 a.m. the C.O., Adjutant and Intelligence Officer made a tour of the line. The whole line was inspected and positions of companies found to be correct. Enemy machine guns and trench mortars were very active, firing on to our line from a position on our right flank, actually in rear of the front line.

Our support line was established on high commanding ground in a series of old trenches for the most part, overlooking the ground in front for some three kilos to the right of and as far as the village of Foucaucourt on our left centre. The enemy had now shortened his barrage and was firing point blank on our line. This, with powerful machine gun and trench mortar fire made it most difficult to further consolidate the line. Our losses up to this time had been fairly heavy.

During the morning Lieut. McGinn reported to me that with a patrol and a 5th Battalion officer he had reconnoitred the long communication trench called Eniecourt Alley to a depth of 800 yards and found no Huns—they had reached the roadway that ran along our front. However, lower down on the right, opposite 'A' Coy. front there was much German activity. I sent this report along to Battalion Headquarters.

At 4 o'clock I received orders from the C.O. that the line was to be advanced as far as we could go towards the village of Foucaucourt in the valley about a mile in front. Zero hour was 4.30 p.m. at which time we started the advance. The platoon under C.S.M. Rice I sent to follow up an old trench system on my extreme right company front and McGinn, with his platoon was to work his way along the centre using the long Eniecourt Alley communication trench as his means of approach. We reached the road running across our front, about 800 yards out without opposistion but away on our right we could see 'A' and 'B' Coys. having a tough time. The Huns were there in force making use of the gullies and an old French trench system that provided splendid defence positions. C.S.M. Rice had made so much progress that he and his platoon were away out in advance of the rest of the Battalion—a very dangerous position if the Huns started counter-attacking. I sent a runner to him ordering him to stop his advance and consolidate.

The 5th Battalion on my left had not advanced with us and therefore we also were in a dangerous position, having an open left flank. I was disturbed by this fact. I did not know if the 5th Battalion were advancing or where they were and whether there were any Huns there or not. We were on a sloping ridge and couldn't see over the other side. Where we were now was in full view of the observing Huns, a nasty position to be in. The Huns must have observed our advance to where we were. I didn't like it a bit. If I sent a patrol to look at what they could see on my left they would have been observed by the Huns and fire brought to bear upon them, so I decided to go and have a look myself. I walked along over the top but only got about 100 yards or so when a Hun artillery battery opened fire—5.9's started falling all round me—I started to get back and take cover but was too late, a shell burst a few yards away from me and I was hit high on the left thigh and sent sprawling, where I lay. My gallant diggers who had been watching me, immediately rushed toward me and carried me to a sheltered spot under a bank. Blood was gushing from the wound and a ligature was necessary so they used a piece of signal wire to make a tourniquet. I heard them say the wound was too big to bandage in the normal way—I would lose my leg.

Shelling now was constant. It was too dangerous to carry me away on a stretcher and they wisely refrained from attempting to do this, so there I lay for four or five hours in a more or less unconscious state. As soon as it was dark enough they carried me away to the Regimental Aid Post.

I came to in Le Havre military hospital where they told me I had been for two or three days and that they were sending me to England. I begged the Sister who was preparing me to go on board the Hospital Ship not to move me, I was in too much pain but she kept to her task saying, 'you will be in a comfortable English Hospital in two or three hours.'

I was one of several hundred badly wounded men laid out on the open deck of the Hospital Ship—there were no nurses on board—our destination was Southampton, normally a short run across the English Channel, but it was not to be. German submarines were active outside Southampton and for fifty hours our ship played about outside, up and down the channel, dodging the German submarines. During that time we had no attention whatsoever. There was a Tommy medical orderly doing what he could to attend to the badly wounded. I called and called to him and eventually he came and I asked him to release the tourniquet as it was hurting me so much. He had one look at my wound and then turned away saying, 'its too awful for me to look at—I can't bear to see it.'

Eventually we made the port and American sailors assisted in carrying us all ashore and laying us out on the wharf. A medical officer moved amongst us reading and checking the necessary particulars attached to the lapel of our tunics. Bending over me he spoke, half to himself saying, 'some mistake, they have put my name here. How in the world did they know I would be on duty here?' I said, 'Joynt is my name, how extraordinary!' We turned out to be distant cousins!

Diary Appendixes

Appendix I: Battle Notes and Messages sent and received by Lieutenant W. D. Joynt during the Battle of Chuignes Valley, 23 August 1918

Operation Orders
—————————

5th & 6th Pltns in line
7th & 8th in Support.
Will attack at dawn.
Disposition of S.R.B. as follows.
8th Bgth in touch with 97th L. Bde.
To Capture Brown line & to exploit &
Capture if possible the Green line.
Will advance two Coys in line.
Supported by 2 Coys in rear in
following order — A Coy on the
R. B Coy on the left. Supported
by D on R & C on Left.
1000 yds frontage for Btn.
advancing in line of Sections at
50 paces interval & 200 paces distance
1 Sec Vickers Machine Guns will
follow in rear of 'D' Coy. and a
Sec of Field Eghs in rear of C. Coy.
1 Coy of Pioneers, across the rear
at 1200 paces distance.
forming up line — will be 500 x
in rear of and approx. parallel with

PROYART ROAD.

Btns will be in position at ZERO.
— 1 hour. — ZERO hour will
be 4.45 AM.

12 Tanks are allotted to Bde and
will walk with forward Btns
watches to be synchronised at 10 pm
after Zero. Tanks will dump
material at R.29.b.2.8 and
R 29 Central & R 29.c.3.4.
Bde Dump for S.A.A. water & R.E.
material at R.26.b.5.2.
Communication will be by runner.
Watch must be kept on flanks
& reports made of all moves ford
Capt will liaison with Coys.
and Btns with Btns

Artillery barrage will rest for
two minutes on Right line and
then 100 yards per 2 minutes for
first 3 lifts then 100 yards lifts
for 3 minutes until Objective line
is gained.

Btn H.Q. & R.A.P. will he established
at R. 28. C. 5. 4. after the Btn
has passed over.
Before ZERO. Btn H.Q. will be at
Q 30. C. 5. 4.
A Contact plane will fly along Final
objective calling at ZERO plus
2 hours.
Should the Btn be drawn in
Red ground flares will be lit at
most advanced line of infantry
posts. — The aeroplanes are
distinguished by rectangular panels,
2ft by 1 on both lower planes
Counter attack aeroplanes will
be constantly in the air after
ZERO hour. The signal to
infantry when the enemy is
preparing counter attacks is
a white Parachute flare
fired in the direction of the
impending attack.
In order to drown noise of tanks

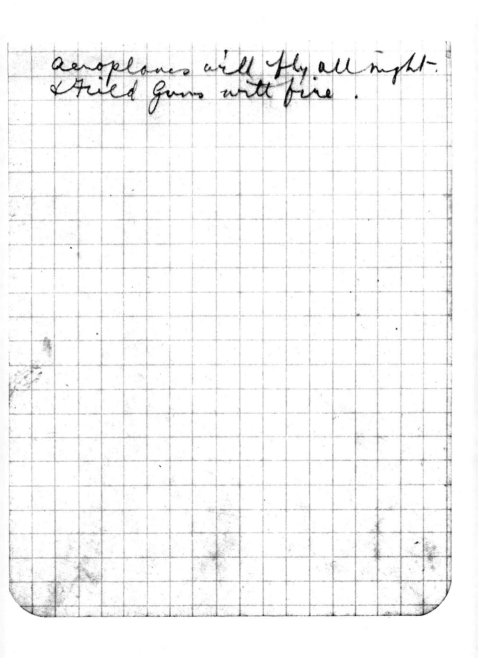

aeroplanes will fly all night.
& Field Guns will fire .

8th Bn

Am on objective at
Eschern left of Bn Sector
The Coy of the 6th fail
to advance —
The Right of our
line appeared to be
doing well early in the
attack, so I went to my
left where I found
6th halted — they show
so little dash that I
pushed on with some of
our men — later I
met Nr. McQuin and we
have just captured the
little Copse at R 30 Central
23rd August stiff fighting

W. A. Joynd Lt
D Coy.

8th Bttn

Am in charge of a
Section of the line on
the left Consisting
about 15 8th Bttn + 20
to 30 6th Bttn — we
line very thinly
AAA Can not find any
other Officers of 6th Bttn
AAA. Enemy are
counter attacking on the
Right

8.50
am
22 Sept

Woodforde Lt
D Coy.

8th Bn

After handing over its sector of the Front Line that I copleted to the 5th & 6th Btm. I withdrew all my men to B Coy HQ. — and I am not about to withdraw further to the Chack Ravine as per your orders received this. B. Coy. AAA.

Captures   150 prisoners
                  1 Field Gun
                  2 Signalling Lamps
                  Several M guns

In the attack on Copse at R 29. Central   Lt McGuir 150/R's + myself captured 100 prisoners after stiff fighting AAA.

In my opinion it was necessary for me to push on + capture this Copse

as the 5ᵗʰ Bat: had advanced
past their objective line
but were being forced
back. — As the 6ᵗʰ Battⁿ
would not push on I
took the initiative and
captured the Copse with
100 prisoners, Other Casualities
were nil. AAH

W.D Joynt Lt
D Coy.

Lt Findley was Killed
before the objective was
taken

8th Bn
—

On reaching Chalk Ravine
C. Spr. Rice informs the OC
your order to move forward
to take up 'A' Coys position
I am moving forward
with the men I have got
to this position immeadiatly
where I will then have
the whole of D Coy. A.A.A
When in position will
forward map location
A.A.A

Chalk Ravine   Wm Joynt Lt

h.40.

D Coy
CASUALITY RETURN

LIEUT FINDLEY   KILLED
80 Pte HEWESTON   "
606 Pte WATSON J.RT. WOUNDED
097 Cpl FERRIE B   "
6363 PTE WATSON R   "
4594 " SMITH A.J.   "
7811 " HUNT W H   "
— " BOWEN L   "
539 " DALTON V.N.   MISSING
" NEWMAN   WOUNDED
1298 " DIDSBURY J   "
6845 " ROBERTS HfW.   "
2810 " WALKER T.J.   "
7601 W. REN R.F.   "
4815 KNOPP W   "
6809 GRACIE A.H.   "
3061 4Cpl GRATTIDGE S   "
6888 PTE PONTER .J.   "
4/cpl BOAKES   POISONED AND
" KING 9c? | 1 OFF. 1 O/R KILLED
DODD 9P? | 16 " WOUNDED
EMMETT | 3 "
                20

D Coy

Strength (approx)

OFFICERS	2
C.S.M. Rice	1
O/Ranks	78
Total Ration Strength :	81 (approx)

[signature] Lt
D. Coy.

23/8/18

C.O. 8th Bttn

The reason for the long delay in effecting change of disposition this afternoon was on account of heavy enemy shelling. Lt. McGuin held up his platoon for an hour AAA. I reported to Col Ulrich as ordered. He seemed greatly surprised at the information that I had a whole Coy in position and said he had not asked for it. AAA. I have three platoons in line & hold from R. edge of Copse to where I am in touch with 5th Bttn on my left AAA I have one platoon in Reserve at Coy H.Q. situated at R.29 D.9.

Could you send up a chap with a paint brush so as to paint men — our friends will

probably until 6 "B" or it.
Overstny chalk marking AAA
the nearest thin point that
I have located is situated
about 100 yds in fort of my
Sector at in the Communication
Fench travelling due EAST
to no mans land, AAA
I have placed blocks in
same trench AAA.
Enemy has registered on
to our line by means of light
flares fired from this post
AAA — Rations plentiful
good quality tonight
AAA — everything else
O.K. AAA

Wd Joynt Lt
D Coy

10.Pm.
23/8/18.

To C.O. 6th Btn

Lieut McGuire who is in
charge of my Section of front
has sent through for retaliation
on a Hun Gun post that
is firing direct on his post
its position is approx M.25 a.2.2.
Could the T.M.S. get on to
the target please? AAA
The enemy artillery is very
active all along our front
and particularly gas shells
at present.

W.D. Joynt Lt
O.C. D Coy
8th Btn

3.40 am.
18/18

C.O. 8TH Bn

Lieut McQuinn + a 5th Bn
Officers have just returned
from reconnoitring the long
straight Communication line
called ENIECOURT ALLEY
to a total distance of 800
yards from my posts at R.30.C.1.
and could gain no touch
with the enemy.

WmJoynt Lt
D Coy.
9th Bn

11.25AM.

24/8/18.

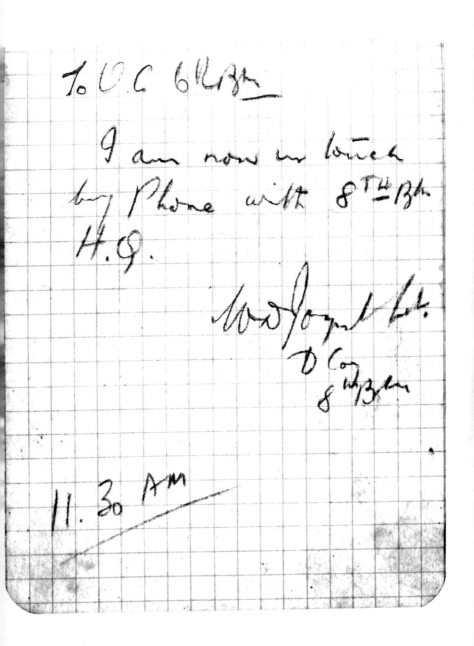

To O C 6th/13th

I am now in touch by Phone with 8th—13th H.G.

11. 30 AM

Intelligence Report

Relief   Relief completed Satisfactly
with A coy of the 6 2 Bn

owing to the very heavy
Gas shell bombardments
necessitating us all having
to keep our Respirators
on I was not able to
write up an Intelligence
Report.

Gas   Gas shells have fallen in
Shell   great numbers all over my
area — and forced us to
wear Gas helmets for over
two hours. —

Intermittent burst of fire
all our Sector from all
Calibres. — and an
Exceptionally number of 77s.
two of byort. 77.

To adjutant.
8th Bn

bm you please get the
Pioneers to make a Cross
for —
  2777 Pte SELLS J.
Killed in a chain To day
by shell fire

also
  — Pte HEWESTON. WH.
Killed in the advance
yesterday with Lt Findley.
Poor old Findley lies
somewhere near 8th Bn HQ
perhaps you can arrange
to have ground searched
this personal effects secured
also Cross — after the relief

24/8/8 .   W Joynt
                    D Coy

Appendix II: Messages sent and received by 8th Battalion

(Message from Forward Brigade H.Q.)

To 8 Battn

Verbal message from 6th Battn
want reinforcements on right
immediately.

Addressed 2nd A.I. Bde repeated
8th Battn.

Time 10.15 a.m.	*From I.O. Forward*
23rd August	*Bde Centre*

URGENT

To Lieut Joynt D. Coy
Reinforce 6th Bn line with all
D. Coy AAA. A Coy are doing
same on 6th Bn right AAA. You
have done well.

Time 11.30 a.m.	*8 Battn*
23rd August	

To all Battns 2 A.I. Bde

Prisoners taken in todays operation
counted in Divisional Cage
exclusive of wounded and stretcher
bearers up to 8.30 p.m. by 2nd Bde

      37 officers
     1229 other ranks

23rd August   *2nd A.I. Bde*

Message from C.O. 8th Battn to 2nd Brigade H.Q.

Secret to 2nd A.I. Bde

I propose to advance my line today
at 4 p.m. to a general line
approximately through M23 A.3.1. M26
C.5.1. then to M26 Central AAA.
Artillery will not be required but
I desire men warned AAA. Please state
if you concur AAA. In any case I shall
advance unless you direct otherwise.

Time 1.24 p.m.   *Signed 8 Battn*

25th August

To 2nd A.I. Bde

*Whole line advanced on an
average 300 yards AAA. Line
now lies on formerly proposed
Green Line running through
M25 Central M25 C.5.2. M31
C.2.8. and in touch with both
flanks.*

Time 7.00 p.m.   *8 Battn*
25th August

To All Coys

*All previous relief instructions
cancelled AAA. 30th Battn will
relieve whole front line AAA.
Guides to be at Battn H.Q. at
8 p.m. AAA. Coys to move out
complete independently and meet
buses at Main Road in rear of
PROYART to be conveyed to Camp
at P.17 A.2.2.*

Time 6.00 p.m.   *8 Battn*
26th August

To 2nd A.I.F. Bde

Relief complete.

Time 12.50 p.m.   *8 Battn*
27th August

Appendix III: Official Reports by Lieutenant-Colonel J. W. Mitchell commanding 8th Battalion A.I.F., of operations during August 1918

The following official reports and the 8th Battalion War Diary for August were obtained from the Australian War Memorial Library, Canberra. These reports, forwarded to the Australian Records Section by the 8th Battalion Commanding Officer, Colonel Mitchell, cover the operations of his battalion during the month of August 1918.

Headquarters,
8 Battalion A.I.F.
9th September 1918

Officer I/C
Aust. War Records Section
London

In forwarding the War Diary for the period of August it will be noticed that the general condition of the Unit is contained for the most part in the narratives.

Despite the fact that the month passed through has been one of the most, if not the most exhausting one of the Battalion history, the men generally speaking have stood the test well. Weary to the point of exhaustion after each battle, the short period of two or three days sleep and quiet has found them ready to continue when required and to carry out their tasks with more than satisfactory results.

Reinforcements have been practically nil, and after the wastage of each battle our strength is at a very low point indeed. So much so that a 3 Coy and 3 platoon organization is imperative which means that half the allotted Lewis Guns are unmanned.

The gallantry, drive, dash and initiative displayed by all ranks in action has been of the highest order and undoubtedly has been the main factor of the Battalion's success in all undertakings.

Engagements have been fierce, distances long and resistance at times particularly fierce and bitter, but at no period was anyone found wanting in the most difficult task.

A glance at the numbers of recommendations for immediate honours and awards alone would convey some idea of the fierce fighting participated in and although a copy of individual gallantry and sacrifice in the face of the biggest odds is not an 'appendix' to the Diary or any narrative annexed it is questionable if it should not be so, since the standard required may not have been reached to gain the highest or any specified distinction by the men concerned.

In my opinion their gallant deeds should not be lost sight of but should be contained in the Diary or other form if not for the future historians, then certainly to facilitate the subsequent history of the Battalion being written.

Signed J. W. MITCHELL Lt.-Col.
Commanding 8th Battalion A.I.F.

Transcription of Narrative of Operations conducted by 8th Battalion A.I.F. from 21st to 27th August 1918 by Lieut-Colonel J. W. Mitchell, Commanding

On 21/8/18 the Battn left tented camp on Somme river bank near HAMEL at 8.30 a.m. leaving a nucleus at Corbie. Lists of officers and men comprising same attached and marched via HAMEL and main Peronne-Amiens Road to dugouts and trenches at Q29.C.2.1. reaching there at 12.45 a.m. on 22nd inst.

The transport less cookers and water carts which remained with Btn proceeded to park at MORCOURT.

The night was exceptionally clear with a brilliant moon shining.

The men were in good spirits, whistling and singing during the whole march and stood the march well.

All ranks were given a hot drink on reaching the new area.

On the morning of the 22nd the C.O., Adjutant and Intelligence Officer proceeded upon reconnaissance to the front line.

Parties were also sent from each Company to view 'forming up' area.

Upon C.O.'s return from Brigade a conference of Coy. Cmdrs. was called. Battle instructions were issued to all and dispositions, equipment etc. were discussed. Coy. Cmdrs.

were shown their exact positions on the actual ground for the attack.

The weather throughout the day was exceptionally hot.

Zero hour for our attack was 4.45 on the morning of the 23/8/18.

At 3.45 all troops were in position in rear of 6 Btn—7th Btn on our left and in touch with 9th Bde (Scottish) on our right.

The Assembly was carried out without incident. Our artillery had been active during the night and many tanks had proceeded to positions, passing our troops en route. The night was very bright, clear and warm.

Our dispositions now were A and D Coys. 500 yards in rear of 6th Bn across the whole Bn front with D on the right and A on the left. Each Company had four platoons in line of Sections with large intervals and distances between. This formation was necessary owing to the large front to be covered and small strength of Battalion. Touch was easily maintained and all ranks had a hot meal before moving off— Cookers remaining at Q 25.d.

Upon the barrage opening with all guns giving a splendid weight of artillery, all infantry, after the first two minutes, moved forward before the barrage lifted. The enemy gave a most magnificent display of flares, many of all colours and shapes being observed. He retaliated (answered) with startling suddenness and accuracy with a powerful barrage on his barrage line, immediately in rear of our old front line since his own posts were so close to our own front line.

After the attacking troops were all in position the line troops were withdrawn and our barrage actually opened on our own evacuated lines, consequently, practically the whole of our troops had to pass through. It was here that Capt. G. G. Johnston and 2/Lieut. L. G. White were killed outright.

The whole action was of such a surprising nature, with intense artillery and tank assistance, that the outposts of the enemy did not attempt to fight, but surrendered freely. Immediately the action commenced, prisoners began to come in and very soon in the day there were more prisoners proceeding to the rear than there were troops going forward.

It was a common sight to see formed bodies of a hundred Huns in charge of one escort, marching to the rear.

At 6 a.m. Bn H.Q. and R.A.P. were established at R 30.C.1.4. when word was received that A, B and C Coys were in position and consolidating and were in touch with the right flank.

D. Coy at this stage was fighting on the left of the 6th Battalion and had been doing so for practically the whole distance.

The Battalion Aid Post lay in the centre of line of evacuation and was rapidly becoming congested with wounded of all units. But, with the aid of improvised stretchers and the free use of prisoners, the post was cleared of casualties by 9 a.m.

The tanks advanced with the barrage and did good work everywhere. The supporting tanks carrying S.A.A. and material reached their appointed dumps O.K.

Two Coys, A and D were drawn into the fight early. D Coy on LIEUT. W. D. JOYNT'S initiative on account of a gap being left in the front line on the 6th Bns left flank and their flank threatened. Also, the 6th Bn had suffered many officer casualties and this part of their line was without experienced leaders. LIEUT. W. D. JOYNT took command of this part of the line and it was due to him that part of HERLEVILLE WOOD and the dugout system of that ravine, containing a Battalion H.Q. and about 70 O.R. was taken and allowed the final objective to be reached.

Then he and LIEUT. McGINN with two platoons of the 8th Bn crossed the road and attacked the trench system in 36 C. This system was solidly held by enemy machine gunners who were firing on the 6th Bn flank and causing many casualties. An enemy aid post was captured here, also a field gun doing anti-tank work. With Lieut. Joynt in Command and Lieut. McGinn skilfully handling his platoon, they worked up the old trenches and surrounded Plateau Wood. This Wood contained a nest of machine guns and about 70 prisoners were taken. This Wood commanded the flank of the 5th Bn on our left and after it was captured allowed their advance to go on unhindered. D Coy of the 8th Bn thus reached the final objective and formed part of the front line. No tanks took part in the capture.

Three officers being killed, three wounded and about 90 O/Ranks killed or wounded. The majority of the wounds were serious, mostly from shell fire though quite a number from bullets.

One section of machine guns was put into position on the right flank in a most commanding position while two Stokes mortars were placed in the support line itself.

Information was now received from the 6th Bn that D Coy of the 8th Btn on their left had gained their objective but were wholly out of touch with the right flank. A Coy of the 8th Btn were ordered to push forward to clear up the situation and maintain touch with the right.

Owing to the heavy fire and the fact that hostile pockets of Huns were still in the valley between our line and the 6th Btn line this movement took some little time and it was not till after midday that the move was completed.

The Company experienced some little difficulty in movement and had to fight practically the whole way. At one point at No. 5 Wood a party of 45 of the enemy came out and surrendered.

The Company succeeded in establishing itself some little distance in rear of the line and in linking up with the Scottish on the right. Our dispositions now were A Coy Line Right, D Coy Line Left (on either side of the 6th Btn) with C and B Coys in Support Line.

Throughout the afternoon the enemy shelled the whole area from the front line to our old front line heavily and many gas shells were fired. At no point along the front held by our two Companies had they penetrated beyond the Brown Line (objective) though practically all along they were established along same.

S.A.A. and bombs were continually being called for and the two support Coys had a busy time carrying forward to supply the front line Company's needs. At about 3 p.m. aeroplanes dropped five cases of S.A.A. on to Support Line.

Throughout the afternoon numbers of enemy aeroplanes —at intervals—flew low over our area firing machine guns and dropping small bombs on our troops. Extremely annoying but doing little actual damage.

Ration limbers arrived at Battalion H.Q. with rations and hot meals for all ranks, in containers, at 8.50 p.m. These went forward as far as Support Line and C and B Coys carried to front line Coys. At 11 p.m. the enemy planes, flying low, dropped bombs over the whole area but paid most attention to the main road.

The day being hot, together with the strain imposed upon the men, caused all water to be consumed. Water was brought up by a limber though later it was discovered that a good supply was obtainable in all the large gullies.

On the 24th, during darkness, A. Coy pushed forward under some resistance by machine guns and bombs from the enemy and advanced their line about 300 yards, working in conjunction with the Highlanders on the Right.

The enemy continued to shell rear areas with short bursts of very heavy fire. Many badly wounded of the enemy were brought in and dressed by our doctor.

At about 3 a.m. the enemy threw gas shells into the Woods and area around Btn H.Q's. Rations arrived at Bn H.Q. at 3 a.m. and all Coys reported meal O.K.

By daylight A. Coy had moved forward and advanced our line past the Brown Line and several machine guns and snipers were mopped up.

The enemy also shelled with H.E. and gas shells, the whole of the newly captured area and evidently expected further advance on our part. By 5 a.m. telephone communication was put through to the front line Coys.

At 9 a.m. the C.O. visited D Coy H.Q. The valleys in the vicinity were still thick with gas after the shelling of the night before. The enemy became very quiet though movement far behind the line of odd troops going back was observed.

The remainder of the day till dusk was quiet. At 5 p.m. notice was received that the 8th Btn would relieve the 6th Btn.

A number of men are being evacuated through the effects of gas, chiefly from the support Coy.

At 10 p.m. the remaining two Coys moved into the front line and the 6th Btn H.Q. taken over by us. Relief was complete by midnight, being hindered by gas shelling in the valleys.

Our dispositions now are all Coys in the line, A, B, C and D reading from Right to Left.

At 1.15 a.m. on the 25th the S.O.S. was sent up about a mile on our right but nothing eventuated.

Throughout the whole of the night the enemy shelled the Woods and valleys with yellow cross and other gas shells. From 5 a.m. the enemy put down another counter preparation and the shelling ceased.

A number of our men are being evacuated through gas.

At 12 noon the Brigadier made a tour of the line, the Adjutant accompanying him. Our batteries were in position by this time and firing continuously.

Though our men could walk around on top, the enemy either did not observe or did not desire to fire. At 2 p.m. officers of the 2nd Btn visited Btn H.Q.

At 4 p.m. an order was issued to all Coys in the front line to push forward to the Green Line if possible.

At 4.15 p.m. the Coys pushed forward, working up the old communication trenches. D. Coy advanced without opposition though A, B and C Coys met with strong opposition from machine gun fire, trench mortars and bombs.

The enemy had bomb stops and much barbed wire in his communication trenches.

On the whole our line was advanced between 200 and 300 yards up to the Green Line.

A great many men's eyes were affected by the gas and our total casualties up to date were five officers and 200 O/R's.

At 7.40 p.m. our 18 pounders shelled with good effect targets in front of our new posts. Our line strength was reduced by this time to 120 all ranks. Through enemy shelling communications were cut with Brigade H.Q. and we were out of touch except by runner for about 9 hours. At 9.15 p.m. heavy rain set in.

At 12 midnight our 18 pounders had a practice shoot on our front.

On the 26th, owing to shortage of officers in the line (1 per Coy) three officers arrived from nucleus. At 4 a.m. the weather became dull and rain set in. The issue of Rum was greatly appreciated.

As usual before dawn, the enemy put down a heavy barrage and soaked the valleys and woods with gas, causing heavy casualties. By 9 a.m. everything became very quiet and hot cocoa and milk was sent up to the line.

Officers of the 56th Btn visited our line in expectation of relief. At 5.45 p.m. one of our balloons was brought down by enemy aeroplanes.

It was now definitely decided that the 30th Btn was to relieve us. Guides from this unit arrived at 10 p.m. and one Coy B. Coy of the 30th Btn relieved the whole front line. The relief went through without a hitch, being completed by 12.50 a.m. on the 27th. After relief, Btn moved out by Coys and embussed on the main road near Proyart and were taken to camp at P.17 A.2.2. in rear of Hamel.

Throughout the action the work of the contact planes was good. Too much praise cannot be given to the tanks, whose assistance was invaluable. Their action aroused the greatest possible enthusiasm among all ranks. The weight and accuracy of our artillery was splendid and counted in a large measure for the entire success of the fight. Many casualties were caused amongst the enemy by our artillery and many prisoners, when taken, appeared stunned by the weight of same. No doubt this was one reason for their lack of fighting, displayed everywhere.

There appears to be little doubt that the enemy's shells of all calibres of H.E. contain gas and that he always combines both ordinary gas shells with H.E. and puts his shots down with startling suddenness. He has, without doubt, adopted a method of Storm Shoots, commencing quickly, and powerfully, and sometimes lasting for hours. The approximate number of shells fired could not hope to be arrived at, though, since every portion of the area was soaked with gas, some thousands must have been fired, going far beyond the 10,000 mark.

Respirators were worn continuously and doubtless saved many men, though burns were prevalent and men's clothing was soaked. Men dozed in their respirators and became ill. All were affected and some 80 evacuations resulted.

It was impossible to push forward the line to escape and since the gentle breeze was towards the enemy, they had, of necessity, to stand it.

The condition of the men going into action was good, they were cheerful and confident. However, the long fight, heat and excitement entailed a great strain upon them and when seen on the Green Line on the afternoon of the 25th, they were exhausted to a degree, all more or less suffering from gas effects, and could not possibly hope to beat off any determined enemy attack. Want of sleep was the most prevalent factor and they were rapidly becoming nervy under the continuous storms of enemy shell fire.

The number of prisoners taken by the 8th and 6th Battalions could not hope to be accurately arrived at though a fair estimate may be given at between 800 and 900 all ranks. Amongst these were two Battalion commanders and four medical officers.

Captures in guns, etc, were 1-77 c.m. tank gun and trench mortars and machine guns were both numerous and distributed over the whole area.

A fair estimate of machine guns in the two Battalion areas is given at 80, both heavy and light, though chiefly of the heavy type.

Sgd. J. W. MITCHELL
C.O. 8 Bn.

Our strength upon going into action was:
30 officers   412 O/ranks

Strength at nucleus:
7 officers   52 O/ranks

Casualties for tour were:
7 officers   240 O/ranks

BATTLE OF CHUIGNES VALLEY
NOMINAL ROLL OF OFFICERS 8TH BATTN
22ND FOR 23RD AUGUST 1918

In the Line

Headquarters

Lt. Col. J. W. Mitchell D.S.O. *Commanding*
Lieut. H. D. Temple M.C. *Assist Adjutant*
Lieut. J. G. Evans *Lewis Gun Officer*
Lieut. A. W. Finlayson M.C. *Signalling Officer*
Capt. P. J. F. O'Shea M.C. *Medical Officer*

A. Coy	*C. Coy*
Capt. G. E. Johnston	Lieut. L. G. Murdock M.C.
Lieut. Anderson D.C.M.	Lieut. H. G. Whitton
Lieut. A. R. McFadyen	C.S.M. E. E. Jones M.M.
Sgt. Eccles D.C.M.	Sgt. H. R. Davis

B. Coy	*D. Coy*
Lieut. D. M. Graham	Lieut. C. Findlay
Lieut. P. G. Perkin	Lieut. W. D. Joynt
Lieut. W. Young M.C. M.M.	Lieut. L. C. McGinn
C.S.M. L. C. White	C.S.M. A. J. Rice

Major J. C. M. Traill D.S.O. M.C. *Liaison Duties*
Capt. R. J. Wallis M.C. *Liaison Duties*

Transport Lines

Capt. E. Freeman *Q.M.*
Lieut. H. Fenton *Assist Q.M.*
Lieut. F. Hickson M.C. *Transport Officer*
Lieut. R. Woodhouse *Messing Officer*

Detached Duties

Lieut C. ———— *Div. Duties*
Lieut. W. G. M. Clarridge *Div. Duties*
Lieut. R. L. Gilmour M.M. *Leave*

PART THREE

The Final Days—
August, September and October 1918

Capture of Mont St Quentin

August 1918

On 21 August 1918, following the successful attacks of the Australian divisions on the Somme, Haig ordered the Third Army, followed later by the First Army with the Canadian Corps as its spearhead, to start an offensive with a view to driving through the northern end of the Hindenberg Line, but without risking too many casualties. At the same time he sent Monash an instruction to 'go easy' and only to engage in patrol encounters, leaving it now to the northern armies to do the attacking. In these operations the latter employed the tactics that were used by the Australians in their 8 August offensive (Germany's Black Day), and soon had the Germans on the run. Nearly the whole British Front now became active. German morale was patchy, and great progress was made. Eventually the left flank of the Hindenberg Line was turned, although the Germans threw in many fresh divisions and fought strongly in some places. However, so low had German morale become that in many instances they surrendered without fighting as soon as their troops were attacked.

Monash, certain that Haig and Rawlinson did not realize what striking power the Australian infantry retained despite several weeks of constant fighting and the casualties they had suffered, seized on the instruction to keep in touch with the enemy to justify his continuing 'an aggressive policy'.

He ordered the 2nd and 5th Divisions to keep up a continual pressure and advance by infiltration, but to avoid fighting that might involve heavy losses. By this means these divisions forced their way into the main section of the German Line of Defence, and further south the Australian 6th Brigade, having been ordered to take whatever ground it could to help the 3rd Division, continued the fighting. The men of the 6th Brigade were so worn out, however, that they had to get assistance from the 8th Brigade under General Tivey (no longer called 'Tivey's Chocolates', their nickname when they first joined the A.I.F. in Egypt) — although they themselves were falling with exhaustion. Nevertheless they were told that they had to capture Cléry, a strongly defended locality covering the approaches to the crossing of the Somme River at Péronne. And this they did, for General Monash had decided next day to harass the Germans so closely that he might rush two brigades across the Somme facing Péronne and then capture the height fronting Mont St Quentin, considered an impregnable fortress protecting the whole of the German Hindenberg Outpost Line. The possession of these heights would open the way to a further plan that Monash had in mind: to capture Mont St Quentin itself. He informed Rawlinson, the Army Commander, of his intentions but got no encouragement. Rawlinson considered that further preparation and the employment of fresher and stronger troops would be needed to successfully carry out such a risky operation.

The two brigades Monash proposed to use were only at about a quarter of their strength due to casualties suffered during the heavy fighting of the previous three weeks. This also applied to all the other Australian divisions, which were completely exhausted and needed resting. Rawlinson and Haig knew this but Monash recognized that the German troops were vulnerable, suffering as they were from the effects of the relentless and continuous — almost daily — attacks by his forces. He persisted with his urging and ultimately Rawlinson consented and reluctantly withdrew his opposition. He did so smilingly but not hopefully, knowing the fatigue and war-weariness the troops were suffering from and the impregnability of the position to be attacked.

At 5 a.m. on 31 August the 5th Australian Brigade of the 2nd Australian Division commenced their attack, followed later by the 6th Brigade, which took over in the afternoon and continued the advance.

It was a brilliant tactical stroke that Monash conceived and carried out. He planned to surprise the enemy by transferring his main strength to the northern side of the Somme and then rushing the heights of Mont St Quentin, which was two miles beyond the river and looked down on the old turreted, ramparted and moated city of Péronne at its southern foot — the recognized key to that position.

As the companies were so light in manpower the leaders of the attacking troops said their best chance of success lay in making as much noise as they could, so the troops advanced yelling and shouting. The cheering platoons ran into the Germans, who seemed bewildered and quickly surrendered. The Australians charged on up the slope and by the time they reached the main German trench line the face of the Mount ahead of them was covered with Germans fleeing over both sides of the hill. The Australians kept on up and over the slope, routing the German supports and reserves.

That morning as he was shaving, General Rawlinson received the astonishing news that the Mount had been captured. Haig was also amazed to learn of Monash's achievement.

The 3rd Division at the same time advanced further north, and next day the 6th Brigade, having passed through the 5th Brigade, seized the summit, and the 5th Division, which had been brought round, captured the woods north of Péronne, crossed the moat and took the main part of the town. Two days later the 7th Brigade (2nd Division) drove beyond the Mount and joined 5th Division in clearing the rest of Péronne.

Monash's plan succeeded after some most extraordinary feats of initiative and daring on the part of junior officers whose men followed them unhesitatingly and, in some cases, needed no leading. Their casualties were heavy, but not when considered in relation to the tremendous boost to Allied morale and the almost total collapse of German resistance from then onwards. The Somme River was crossed and Péronne and other heights captured.

According to Bean, the attack on Mont St Quentin

> . . . was in some ways the most formidable ever faced by Australian infantry. Mont St Quentin was already a familiar sight; it had faced the attacking battalions most of the day before; as they came over the Cléry Bridge it backed the centre of the landscape, resembling an old man's pate, shallow, completely bald except for the village trees rising in a tousled tuft above the forehead, and trenches and bands of rusty wire seaming like wrinkles the bare glacis below . . .
>
> All knew the Mount to be a famous fortress of the Western Front, and as the hour of the barrage, 5 o'clock, drew near few officers or men in the tired companies . . . averaging only 60 rifles . . . believed they had any chance of success.*

Bean also wrote that 'The impression everywhere made by the capture of Mont St Quentin would have been even greater had those who heard of it realized the number and condition of the troops that achieved it'. Eight very tired battalions, each comprising only some 350 rifles with a handful of machine gunners and four companies of less than 100 men each captured 500 prisoners and met and conquered

---

* Bean, vol. vi, pp. 809-10.

a force far greater than their own in well entrenched positions and with machine guns sweeping the approaches.

However, Barrie Pitt writes in his book *1918 — the Last Act:*

> It [the capture of Mont St Quentin] cannot be said to have been a satisfactory day's battle, especially in comparison with those which had immediately preceded it — which possibly accounts for the defiant air about the paragraph in the Fourth Army History which sums it up: 'The Attack on Mont St Quentin by the 5th Brigade, with only hastily arranged artillery support and without a creeping barrage, ranks as one of the most notable examples of pluck and enterprise during the war.'

Unfortunately, pluck and enterprise are not enough in battle.*

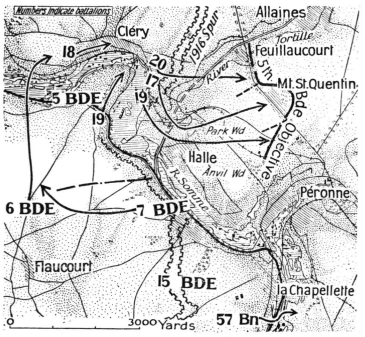

Monash's plan for the capture of Mont St Quentin

* Pitt, p. 216.

America Joins In

On 19 September Foch asked for the two American divisions in G.H.Q. Reserve that had not yet done any fighting to join a British General Offensive against the Hindenberg Line. These two divisions were to attack as a corps but the commander, Major-General Read, placed himself under General Monash and allowed him to control the American divisions directly, thus temporarily eliminating himself from tactical control. This was a generous gesture on the part of the American commander. Major-General Read also suggested that an Australian Mission be formed whose role would be to act as a body of expert advisors on all questions of tactical technique. This suggestion was warmly accepted by General Monash and advisers were selected from the Australian 1st and 4th Divisions. Capt. R. Wallis, Adjutant of the 8th Battalion, was one of those appointed and he afterwards told the author that the American commander of the unit he was working with said to him that the Americans were not worried much if they suffered casualties because that fact would bring home to their nation that they (the American soldiers) were really helping to win the war.

General Monash wrote:

> ... I had been called upon to undertake the responsibility of directing in a great battle two Divisions (the 27th &

30th) of United States troops, numbering altogether some 50,000 men ... It was certainly anomalous that a whole organised Corps should pass under the orders of a Corps Headquarters of another nationality, but ... General Rawlinson relied on the good sense and mutual forbearance of the two Corps Commanders concerned ... the arrangement caused me no anxiety or difficulty. General Read and his staff most readily adapted themselves to the situation.*

These Americans were full of enthusiasm but sadly lacking in battle experience. They were also very short of officers as so many were away attending schools of instruction. The result was that the attacking Americans in their keenness rushed foward over and over again past their objectives and failed to 'mop up' behind them, enabling the Germans to re-emerge from their dugouts and attack the advancing troops from the rear, causing a lot of unnecessary casualties.

* Monash, pp. 242-3.

Haig Issues New Instructions

At this stage the First and Third British Armies were advancing so slowly in comparison with the successful operations being conducted by the Australians that Haig decided that from now on a different method of attack would be adopted by all British forces, as the German Army was showing signs of decay and demoralization. His Order, recorded in the official history, ran:

> To turn the present situation to account the most resolute offensive is everywhere desirable. Risks which a month ago would have been criminal to incur ought now to be incurred as a duty. It is no longer necessary to advance in regular lines and step by step. On the contrary each division should be given a distant objective which must be reached independently of its neighbour and even if one's flank is thereby exposed for the time being.
>
> Reinforcements must be directed to points where our troops are gaining ground, not where they are checked... The situation is most favourable. Let each one of us act energetically, and without hesitation push forward to our objective.*

Accordingly, the British First and Third Armies pierced the German Line towards Cambrai, and Rawlinson, encouraged by this success in the north, then obtained leave to prepare a full dress attack on his own front by British

* Bean, vol. vi, p. 761.

and Australian troops on 18 September. This allowed a fortnight's preparation.

A formidable spot on the way to this attack on the Hindenburg Line was the village of Hargicourt, strongly defended by the Germans. However, this was quickly overcome and captured by the 1st Australian Division which, coming back into the line after two weeks rest, carried both its objectives. The capture of this village meant the mastering of the whole of the Hindenberg Outpost Line. The 1st Division was assisted by the 4th Australian Division, which exploited the attack by capturing the third objective on its southern flank, taking many prisoners and routing hundreds more.

Rawlinson's general offensive which followed was a huge success. The ten assaulting divisions, eight English (or British) and two Australian, took 12,000 prisoners and 100 guns. Of these the two depleted Australian divisions captured 4,300 prisoners and 76 guns at a cost of 1,260 casualties, and thrust far beyond either of the British corps operating on their flanks.

General Rawlinson reported to General Haig that captured German officer prisoners had said their men would not now face the Australians.

Gregory Blaxland has this to say in his book *Amiens 1918* concerning the activities of the A.I.F. at this time:

> The Australians had set the pace and by their example inspired others. Since their arrival at Villers-Bretonneux they had established a supremacy over the enemy which must be without equal for any such sustained period of fighting in the history of war. They were famous, of course, for their initiative, audacity and superb fieldcraft, but Monash was well aware that they would not make full use of their skills without confidence in their commanders and this in turn depended on thorough and imaginative planning.*

* Blaxland, p. 243-4.

The Final Battle

There was only one obstacle left — beyond that there were no more established German lines of defence. This was the village of Montbrehain, on a plateau that dominated any further advance. Its capture on 4 October by the 2nd Division with the 6th Brigade leading proved to be the final major battle on that section of the front because on the next day the Germans asked for the terms of an Armistice. The total captures exceeded 1,000 prisoners, an astonishing performance for three very weak brigades that two days later took another 800 prisoners. By nightfall on 5 October the task of the 2nd Division and also of the Australian Corps was completed and steps taken to hand over the Corps Front to the 27th and 30th American Divisions which had now been reorganized and rested. Their own Corps Commander, General Read, took over that section of the front. The Australian Corps was withdrawn to a back area behind Amiens near the French coast for a well-earned rest and for reorganization.

A Welcome Rest; 4th Army's Appreciation and Tribute

During that very welcome rest, members of the Australian Corps received the following letter from General Rawlinson, commanding the British Fourth Army:

"Since the Australian Corps joined the 4th Army on the 8th April, 1918, they have passed through a period of hard and uniformly successful fighting of which all ranks have every right to feel proud.

"Now that it has been possible to give the Australian Corps a well-earned period of rest, I wish to express to them my gratitude for all that they have done. I have watched with the greatest interest and admiration the various stages through which they have passed, from the hard times of Flers and Pozières to their culminating victories at Mont St Quentin and the great Hindenburg system at Bony, Bellicourt Tunnel and Montbrehain.

"During the summer of 1918 the safety of Amiens has been principally due to their determination, tenacity and valour.

"The story of what they have accomplished as a fighting Army Corps, of the diligence, gallantry and skill which they have exhibited, and of the scientific methods which they have so thoroughly learned and so successfully applied, has gained for all Australians a place of honour amongst nations and amongst the English-speaking races in particular.

"It has been my privilege to lead the Australian Corps in the 4th Army during the decisive battles since August 8 which bid fair to bring the war to a successful conclusion at no distant date.

"No one realizes more than I do the very prominent part that they have played, for I have watched from day to day every detail of their fighting, and learned to value beyond measure the prowess and determination of all ranks.

"In once more congratulating the Corps on a series of successes unsurpassed in this great war I feel that no mere words of mine can adequately express the renown that they have won for themselves and the position they have established for the Australian nation, not only in France, but throughout the world.

"I wish every officer, N.C.O. and man all possible good fortune in the future and a speedy and safe return to their beloved Australia.

"(Signed) H. RAWLINSON,
"General Commanding 4th Army."

"HEADQUARTERS, 4th ARMY,
"October 20, 1918."

Germany asks for an Armistice

The Germans continued their request for the terms of an Armistice, for the enemy had no defence line left in France. His retreat became general along his whole front and gathered momentum day by day, enabling the Second and Fifth Armies in the north to advance and occupy Lille and the adjacent industrial area of Flanders *without fighting.*

The Armistice negotiations dragged on and uncertainty existed as to when they would be satisfactorily concluded.

On 5 November the Australian Corps again moved up to the front, the 1st and 4th Divisions leading the way, followed by the other three divisions. General Monash established his headquarters at Le Cateau, the very chateau that had been occupied by the German general commanding the 2nd German Army, against which the Australian Corps had been operating for so long. But the very day that Monash arrived there, on 11 November, the order came to cease hostilities.

The war was over and the Australians had seen it through to the very end.

And so, less than eight weeks after the launching of the offensive on 8 August by the Australian and Canadian Corps with the 3rd British Corps on the flank, the Germans were suing for an Armistice. It was also only nine weeks since the Allies had started to prepare for another year of warfare.

In July, three weeks before the 8 August offensive, when Sir Henry Wilson, representing the War Office, and Field Marshal Haig and Marshal Foch held a conference to discuss future war plans, the opinion was expressed that the war would continue throughout 1919. Sir Henry Wilson said 1920!

And how accurate was General Monash's forecast in his special 'Order of the Day' issued on 7 August 1918, that the story of the exploits of the Australian Corps in the impending battle on the Somme would 're-echo throughout the world, and . . . live forever in the history of our home land'.

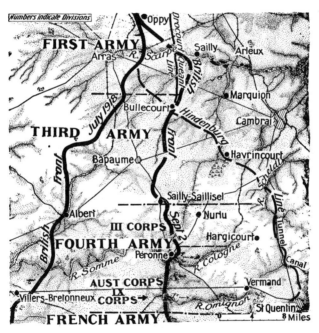

The British Front at the start of the advance to the Hindenburg Line, 5th September 1918

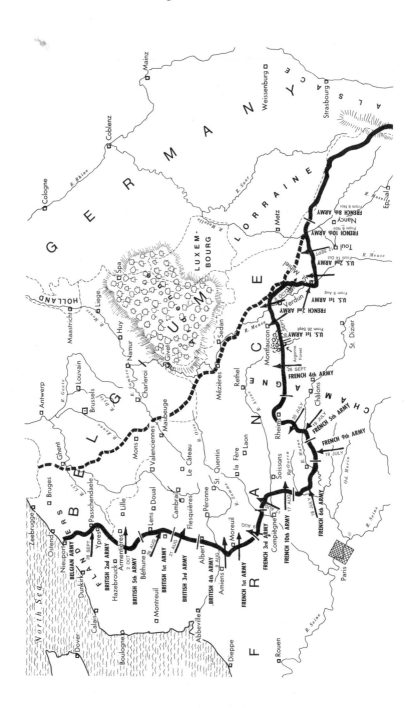

Tributes to a great leader, Sir John Monash

In view of at least one more winter campaign, rumour had it that the British Prime Minister, Lloyd George, was about to appoint Sir John Monash to supersede Marshal Haig. But because there was great opposition from the High Command, which loathed the idea of giving high military positions to civilian soldiers, particularly colonials, he was waiting for a suitable time to make this appointment.

Mr W. M. Hughes, Prime Minister of Australia, said of Monash, 'He was the only General with whom I came into close contact who seemed to me to give due weight to the cost of victory.'

Field-Marshal Viscount Montgomery wrote in his book *A History of Warfare* 'I would name Sir John Monash as the best General on the Western Front in Europe; he possessed real creative originality, and the war might well have been over sooner, and certainly with fewer casualties, had Haig been relieved of his command and Monash appointed to command the British Armies in his place.'

The spirit of the A.I.F. soldier and his high morale

Many have remarked on the high morale of the Australians in battle at this time when they were worked so continuously and suffered such heavy casualties and fatigue. Particularly impressive was their willingness to return to the firing line after only very short periods of rest and carry out fresh attacks with enthusiasm. This was at a time when their only reinforcements consisted of the returning sick and wounded from the hospitals in England. Their cheerfulness and eagerness when ordered to attack again with such weak forces—units down to only about a quarter of their normal strength—was a source of wonder as to what inspired them.

One answer to this question was the Digger's pride. He knew he was definitely doing something to win the war. He had proved his ascendancy over the Hun, whom he invariably defeated. He knew the enemy was frightened of him and would run before him. He was a volunteer, not a conscript, and had enlisted of his own free will to go to the help of the Mother Country, and now he was showing Britishers that the blood he had inherited from his ancestors still ran true. He had a tradition of loyalty to the maxim that one Britisher was as good as two foreigners and so, while still able, he would carry on building up for Australia a reputation as a fighting man.

He also knew that many Englishmen from General Haig down to privates criticized him for his lack of discipline. This was very much mistaken belief, founded on a different conception of what the word 'discipline' meant.

To the Australian discipline meant an unquestioning obedience to all orders received from his superior officers and loyalty to their legitimate commands; it also meant the carrying-out of the intentions of the 'Order of Battle'; orderliness, and respect for authority. All these functions were scrupulously performed by the Australian Digger. In my own experience I know of no case of neglect on the part of the men to obey an order received. This was largely the result of the respect that the Australian soldier held for rank, and felt personally for his superior officer from the company commander down to junior officers (largely recruited from the ranks). Whereas the English Army concentrated on barrack square drill, the Australian Army only gave sufficient time to this work to enable troops to manoeuvre and move about in correct formation.

Generally speaking, the word discipline to the English soldier had a different meaning from that of the dictionary. It meant to him absolutely correct handling of arms and smartness on parade; jumping to attention and the clicking of heels in the presence of an officer; scrupulous saluting (not just saluting, but saluting correctly according to the wording in the Drill Book), not only on parade but off parade as well, even in the streets of London. As an example of what I mean: whilst standing in the crowd watching the Australians marching through London on Anzac Day, a Tommy next to me suddenly shouted for all to hear, 'Look at their rotten discipline', pointing to an occasional slightly incorrect angle in the slope of the rifle of a Digger.

The character of the Digger was so different from that of the Tommy. The average English working man grew up and spent his life in the area immediately surrounding his place of birth. It was said that few if any villagers had even journeyed as far as their adjoining county, their whole life being spent in just doing what they had been told to do and meeting only their working companions. Whereas it was typical of the Australians that they were no sooner in a new place than they were on speaking terms with the local people, even knowing the whereabouts and names of surrounding villages and places up to ten miles from where they were billeted. A story went the rounds of the Diggers that a party of them, out walking the day following their arrival in a back area, met a Tommy from an English regiment camped nearby and asked him the name of the village opposite. The Tommy answered, 'Don't know, Chum, we have only been here for a month'!

Haig stated in May 1918: 'The Australian is a different individual now from when he came to France, both in discipline and smartness'. But Australian soldiers were no different: it was only the viewpoint of British officers that was different, for in all the history of war there is no more signal example of obedience to orders (for that is what discipline should mean) than that shown by the men of Anzac at the Landing and throughout the Gallipoli Campaign. What better example could you find than that shown by the Australian divisions and the Australian Light Horse Brigades at the Evacuation? Casualties expected were 20,000: one man was hurt, whilst getting into a boat.

The view expressed by a famous British General that 'the Australian may prove a great fighter but will never make a soldier' was typical of some opinions expressed by 'higher-ups' when we arrived in France, but before the war was over this view became very much modified. A very senior British officer's comment when I mentioned this saying to him was, 'What rot!' Nevertheless, this false legend about lack of discipline, born out of a feeling of jealousy, pursued the A.I.F. throughout the whole war and since.

PART FOUR

Epilogue

Armistice Celebrations in London, 11 November 1918

I had just started my convalescent leave from hospital and was in Manchester when, with a suddenness that left most of us dumb, a news flash told us that the Germans had signed the terms of an Armistice—it was 11 November 1918. Peace came quite unexpectedly, as most people in England had resigned themselves to at least another year of war.

I immediately hurried back to London to take part in the celebrations. At first the city was comparatively quiet but with Australian Diggers in the lead the crowd surged to Buckingham palace. No sign of the King could be seen. A Digger climbed up on the statue of Queen Victoria exactly opposite the Palace and, sitting in the lap of the statue with a stick in his hand, he beat time to the shouting of the crowd: 'We want the King! We want the King!' Eventually the King appeared with Queen Mary and waved to the crowd, acknowledging their applause. Such a scene was unprecedented in the history of royalty, and it formed a pattern for subsequent royal occasions. We owe that practice to an Australian, reported one of London's newspapers.

As the day wore on the excitement grew but the real outburst of rejoicing did not take place until the next day, thousands having arrived in the city to swell the parading crowd. All, however, was orderly. I was able to book in at the Australian Officers' Club in Piccadilly but we were all soon out on the street. Right throughout the night, until break of day, the crowd surged up and down the streets of London, up Whitehall past the Admiralty Arch, through Trafalgar Square along the Strand, back to Piccadilly Circus and down Haymarket back to Trafalgar Square. It was a sight never to be seen again—we had won the war.

Towards midnight someone started a fire on the base of the Nelson Monument in Trafalgar Square. A big New Zealander took charge and from high up on the structure he kept calling to the crowd below to 'come and feed the flames', and they truly did. Anything made of wood was torn down, including the long side signs on the London buses. A whole pile of wooden blocks coated in tar were thrown on the fire from a nearby roadway dump. As black-out restrictions were still in force, the flames of the tar-covered blocks illuminated the whole of the square and surrounding streets. The excitement of the cheering crowds was terrific. Some of the papers next day blamed the Australians for desecrating the memorial—never, of course, the New Zealanders! Although the heat of the fire caused some cracks in the stone foundations, later examination by engineers indicated that the cracks were no danger to the monument itself.

Years afterwards, when English enthusiasm for Australia had died down, I read a paragraph in a London newspaper referring to the way the Australians celebrated the signing of the Armistice by attempting to burn down England's greatest war memorial!

But the attitude of English civilians towards Australian troops throughout the war and afterwards could not have been warmer. They threw their homes open to men on leave and did much to show their appreciation.

They feted the Australian Prime Minister, Mr William Morris Hughes, some even going so far as to say they wished he could be prime minister of Great Britain.

The Australian March through London

After the signing of the peace terms, while Australian troops were waiting to be repatriated, the press called for some public recognition by the English people of their gratitude for what Australia had done in coming to the aid of Britain in her trouble. A march through London was suggested, at which the people of London could express their appreciation.

This idea was carried out on Anzac Day 1919 followed later by a luncheon for 300 Australian troops given by the Lord Mayor of London at the Guild-hall.

Instead of participating in the march with the 5,000 officers and men detailed, I decided that it would be an event far more interesting for me to watch, and this I started out to do.

I went to Trafalgar Square to see the march but the crowd was so dense that I decided to get into the Underground and proceed to Mansion-house Station. I thought I would have a better view of the march from that vicinity.

At Temple Bar, the old-time gate to the entrance to the City, the medieval ceremony was carried out as the marching Australians approached. The Sheriff of London with his guard halted the column with the challenge: 'Halt, who comes there? Advance one and give the password.' The Australian commander advancing replied: 'Australian troops

wishing to enter the City.' 'Pass Australian troops, all's well,'
replied the Sheriff.

The crowd was thick as I made my way to the square in
front of the Mansion-house and I found a suitable place
in which to stand impossible to find but the area on the far
side of the square had been kept free of people. There was
no one alongside the Mansion-house itself. That would be
a splendid place to see the march, I thought, so I strode
across the square. When halfway over I was followed by a
policeman, who chased after me saying, 'You can't go there.'
I replied, 'I am going to the Mansion-house.' 'Sorry sir',
he said as he saluted, and I continued on my way. Reaching
the far side of the square I stopped and looked back. I was
conspicuously alone and opposite me there were thousands
of people looking on. How dreadful, I thought, I can't stay
here to be pulled back in front of all those people! What
was I to do? Behind me was a side door of the Mansion-
house with a bell on it. I pressed the button and shortly
the door opened. A footman ran his eye over me and bowed
me in, saying, 'The Lady Mayoress and her party are up in
the balcony.' He led the way and I followed him upstairs.
The footman took me to the Lady Mayoress, who held out
her hand saying, 'Welcome, come and stand beside me',
which I did. There were some men but mainly women
looking out from the balcony as the Australian troops entered the square preceded by all the aldermen and sheriffs
of the City of London, who took up their position below as
the Australians with fixed bayonets 'at the slope' marched
past with bands playing.

The women, who I presumed were the wives of the
aldermen and councillors of the City of London and some
of the Royal Palace ladies, were tremendously excited and
kept repeating the nicest things, commenting on the appearance of the Australian troops: 'Aren't they magnificent!'
'Don't they look fine!' One woman in an outburst of en-

Lt.-Gen. Sir John Monash, G.O.C., The Australian Corps, leading the march of 5,000 Australian troops invited by the Lord Mayor of London to parade through the city as a farewell gesture. *Source:* A.W.M.

Part of the Australian contingent with rifles at the slope and fixed bayonets, assembling for the great march through London, a courtesy gesture by the City of London. Only two regiments in the entire British Army have this honour of marching through the City with fixed bayonets.

(*Left*) The Australian Prime Minister, Mr W. M. Hughes, and the Prince of Wales take the salute of the marching Australians. The Lord Mayor of London took the salute in front of the Mansion House. *Source:* A.W.M.

The Victory March of allied troops through London. The British public
gave the Australian section a tremendous reception, as this cheering crowd
(above) in Knightsbridge indicates. *(below)* Australian and other Dominion
farmers at afternoon tea, by invitation, at the King's Farm, Sandringham,
after being shown over the farm. The author, third from the end, left row,
is conversing with two local newspaper reporters. *Source:* Sport & General
Press Agency Ltd.

The author prior to his Investiture at Buckingham Palace by King George V, 11 July 1919.

France showed her appreciation of the Australians with a march through Paris at the invitation of Monsieur Clemenceau, the Premier, and his government.

A troop of Australian Light Horse ready to join the great victory march through London. *Source:* **A.W.M.**

Further examples of British hospitality were encountered when Australian farmers who had served in the war were invited on a tour of English farms *(above)* and to the Jersey Island Agricultural Show *(below)*.

Scene in Horseferry-Road, London, the entrance to Administrative Headquarters was on the right. On the left were the "War Chest" Club (maintained by gifts from Australia, the A.I.F. Clothing Store, and the offices of the War Records Section.
Source: A.W.M.

(*Above*) Nurses of No. 1 Australian General Hospital, Rouen, 23 September, 1918, where the Author was admitted severely wounded before being transferred to England in August 1918. The matron (Miss E. Cornwell) is in the centre of the group, a wonderful band of dedicated women.
(*Right*) Australians in Great Britain attending a special service at Westminster Abbey.
Source: A.W.M.

The Victory March in London, as the author saw it from a window of a house in Belgrave Square.

The Lord Mayor and Sheriffs of the City of London entertain about 300 officers of the A.I.F. including Lieut.-Gen. Sir John Monash and the popular General Birdwood ('Birdie') at a farewell luncheon at the Guild Hall. *Source:* A.W.M.

thusiasm kept saying, 'Don't they look men! Now I know why our girls are going mad over them'.

As I watched the column march by in fours, I saw for the first time a distinct pattern. They all looked the same. Each row of four gave the impression of exactly the same caste of feature—square-jawed, firm of mouth, all with the same look of determination as they marched strictly to attention, eyes to the front and heads erect. The cheering of the crowds below filled me with pride that I also was an Australian. London was certainly giving them a hero's welcome.

After the march all the aldermen, preceded by Edward, Prince of Wales, and the Lord Mayor, came upstairs and I turned to go. I approached the Lady Mayoress to bid her farewell. 'You will stay for lunch,' she said, and we all proceeded into the dining room. I was sat at the centre table, exactly in front of the Prince. On either side of me were distinguished personages to whom I was introduced as 'the Australian'.

After luncheon as the guests departed I thanked the Lady Mayoress for her hospitality and she said, 'Will you sign my book?'

'I have already done that,' I replied.

'No, I mean my own private book,' she said. 'That's the general one you have signed.' She took me into her boudoir and I signed as requested, feeling deeply honoured.

As I stood on the steps of the Mansion-house with the other guests while the Prince of Wales walked down and got into his carriage, the troop of Life Guardsmen forming the Prince's escort was suddenly called to attention by the Escort Commander. He gave the command 'eyes right' and with his sword saluted. The man standing next to me said, 'That's for you, it's Australia we are honouring today.'

As the escort moved off I walked down the steps and mingled with the crowd. I felt the emotion of the day's events into which, without any planning, I had inadvertently walked. It was some time before I regained my composure.

That evening the Australian High Commissioner, Mr Andrew Fisher, gave a reception at Australia House to which I was invited. During the evening I discussed the day's events with Mr Fisher. He told me that when strong support was indicated in favour of the suggestion in the press that Australians march through the City of London to be given a farewell gesture and send-off before returning home to Australia, he approached the War Office with the proposition, but they would not have anything more to do with the idea. He told me he got nowhere with them. He then decided to go direct himself to the Lord Mayor of London and put the proposal to him. The Lord Mayor was most enthusiastic and said 'not only will Australians march through the City of London, but they will march through with bands playing and bayonets fixed.' This was a privilege that only two regiments in the whole of the British Army held. I asked Mr Fisher what the War Office did then and he replied, 'They wiped their hands of the whole affair and let Australian Headquarters and myself make our own arrangements for the march without their assistance.'

The Peace Conference

We all followed with the greatest interest reports of the efforts of our Prime Minister, Mr W. M. Hughes, to combat the dominating views of the American President Mr Woodrow Wilson, who had seemingly taken charge of the Peace Conference.

It appears that Hindenberg and Ludendorff, with the Kaiser's concurrence, realizing that victory to the Germans now seemed remote following Germany's Black Day, 8 August 1918, communicated with the American President and asked him to discuss with the Allies the Armistice terms that they would agree to. In reply he submitted to the Germans a fourteen-point proposition that would be acceptable to them. This was the start of the negotiations that led to the Armistice on 11 November 1918.

Some of these points were quite unacceptable to Mr Hughes, who now found that Australia had no voice on the Peace Council, although in 1915 the British Government had promised Australia that when the time came for peace terms to be discussed Australia would be given the opportunity to have a say and express her views *'in the spirit as well as the letter'* but now that the time had come, the British Government in effect repudiated this agreement.

Mr Hughes in a speech in London strongly objected to some of the Fourteen Points and said plainly that Australia would not be bound by adverse arrangements made by the Peace Conference.

Previously, in the August and September following Germany's Black Day, Mr Hughes, who was greatly impressed by the part played and the victories won by Australians in defeating the Germans, prepared his ground by inviting parties of British press leaders to visit Australian Corps Headquarters and follow the advances of the corps, even showing them personally over the ground won. He did this so that Australia's great achievements in helping to bring about the final days of the war should be known in Great Britain, and to ensure that Australia's voice would be heard in the peace negotiations—also as a counter to the lack of official publicity on the Australians' achievements. Then at the end of October, sensing the imminent collapse of Germany, he rushed off to Paris to support the French in combating any weakening of future terms that might be put up by Mr Wilson. This effort pleased Clemenceau very much and later secured his support generally in the fight that raged to secure for Australia and the other dominions a fair representation at the peace table. Eventually it was agreed that the great powers would have five votes each, Australia and Canada two each and New Zealand one vote, but these votes would not be in addition to the total British vote. This win for the dominions was undoubtedly due entirely to Mr Hughes's personal efforts.

A big bone of contention was Wilson's determination that Germany's colonies should remain in the Allies' sole control. Australia and others wanted straight-out annexation by adjoining powers. New Guinea, captured by Australia, was needed for protection from outside attack and she would not agree otherwise. She captured the territory and wished to hold it; she deserved it if only for her efforts in the war. A stalemate ensued but was eventually solved by a suggestion from Mr John Latham, an Australian lawyer accompanying Sir Joseph Cook, Australian Minister for the Navy, who had come over from Australia to take part in the peace negotiations. This suggestion, ultimately accepted by the conference, was for Australia to have a mandate giving her complete control. This sole mandate would be sufficiently effective, some pointed out, and give Australia the protection she needed. Mr Hughes still refused to agree but ultimately was forced to give way. New Zealand supported Australia, as also did Canada.

At one stage in the negotiations Mr Wilson threatened to resign and return to America but, realizing that the eastern states of America were very pro-British and that would be an unpopular move on his part, he changed his mind and decided to stay on.

At times the wrangle between Hughes and Wilson became so great that the newspapers gave full reports of it that we, on Salisbury Plains, read avidly.

In London where Mr Hughes often appeared in the course of performing public duties he got tremendous receptions, at time with standing ovations. With the British public Australia was tops.

In some quarters, of course, Hughes became unpopular because of his forthright attitude and 'down to earth' manner of speech but we Australians in the camps became very proud of him.

We all wondered why Wilson should have so much power and be chairman of the League of Nations when his country had not suffered overmuch in the war. America had only fought a few battles in the last few weeks of the war and her navy had not done much actual fighting.

As guest of a friend I was taken over the secret Naval Operations Planning Room near Southampton. It was a most interesting experience. The whole of the world's seas were set out in the form of a map spread out on a huge table

and every German submarine or ship that had been destroyed was pinpointed by a marker. Outside Portsmouth
Harbour were hundreds of markers showing the intensity of
the German submarine attacks on British shipping.

The American Navy was also engaged in chasing down
German submarines and I asked the Royal Navy officer
showing me round how many German submarines were
destroyed. When I inquired how many the Americans had
killed he replied 'None.'

The following are reprints of newspaper articles written
at the time of the Peace Conference and give a summary of
the proceedings of the 'Big Ten' at the Conference Table
in Paris.

The first article gives prominence to the attitude and
statements of Mr W. M. Hughes, Prime Minister of Australia, over the repudiation by the conference of promises
made to Australia early in the war. It drew attention to
the work of the A.I.F. in saving Amiens and the resulting
support of France for Mr Hughes's denunciation of the
suggested terms dealing with the German colonies; and it
referred generously to the work of the A.I.F. in the following terms:

> . . . the men and women of France, and, I may add, the
> men of the British Army, too, will allow free speech to the
> spokesman of those who saved the day, and saved the
> campaign on that awful day to the east of Amiens not yet
> a year ago. Was that an occasion when there was time to
> wait for a mandate from some tribunal in the clouds?
> 'Those men are dead. It seems now that the procedure for
> which they gave their lives was all wrong.'

The second article, reprinted from the Paris paper *Le Matin*,
is an account of an interview by the French correspondent
M. Lauzanne with Mr Hughes, and is similar in expression
to that given by Hughes later in England when he was

given such an overwhelming reception by his London audience. Referring to the sacrifices made by Australians the article quotes Hughes as saying:

It is sometimes said that those who were far off did not understand at once in 1914 the grandeur of the cause for which the world was tearing itself to pieces. We were far off and we understood at once. It was not half way through the struggle that we hastened to the defence of civilization.

We had a population of 5,000,000 men and we armed a tenth of them. From the beginning until the end of the tragedy we had six fighting divisions on the front without counting one in Asia Minor. We suffered heavier losses than the whole of America; 255,000 of our sons were either killed, crippled or wounded . . . it was an Australian division that assisted to fill the breach, re-weld the line, and save Amiens.

PEACE CONFERENCE
AND THE
FUTURE EUROPE

EASTERN PROBLEMS

On Saturday the Press Bureau issued the following:

PARIS, Saturday.

The President of the United States of America, the Prime Ministers, and Foreign Ministers of the Allied and Associated Powers, and the Japanese representatives met this afternoon, at the Quai d'Orsay, from three p.m. to 6.15 p.m.

The Conference approved the text of the provisional agreement between the Czechs and the Poles proposed by the delegates of the Powers regarding the Teschen district.

The instructions to be given to the Inter-Allied Commission which is to proceed to Poland were definitely decided upon and approved.

The Roumanian delegates, M. Bratiano and M. Misu, were then introduced. M. Bratiano made a detailed statement of Roumanian claims.

The next meeting will take place on Monday, at eleven a.m.

AUSTRALIA AND MANDATE

MR. HUGHES'S REPUDIATION

From PERCEVAL LANDON

PARIS, Sunday.

Those who have been following with attention the course of the Conference will by this time be in a position to estimate the relative importance of the work which is now being done by it. Considerable success has been obtained in the matter of delimitation of the new frontiers. That is to say, where a dispute has arisen between one of the newly created Central European States and another, there has been shown an excellent spirit of submission to the opinion of the Great Powers, which have permitted them to come into being. But the Powers, even in these cases, have come to no hasty decision. They have been content to appoint a Commission to carry out the work in detail. These Commissions stand in the same relation to the Council of Ten as do the committees appointed to consider and report upon the larger matters of principle that have as yet come before the notice of the Council. It is a good augury for the success of the Peace Conference if the Ten shall continue to allow the local knowledge of the expert to humanise and render possible the idealism which necessarily tends to impair somewhat the practical value of their own decisions. But it cannot have escaped the notice of readers that this harmony reigns especially in minor matters.

From the French point of view the most important matters with which the Conference will deal, that is those affecting France herself, have not yet been reached. But as citizens of the world, nothing that can affect the success of this great attempt to make wars to cease can be without interest to them. With characteristic shrewdness, they have put their finger on the weak spot of the present position. It was a mistake to have announced that the days of secret diplomacy were over. Had the advisability—which is now not denied—of maintaining some kind of restraint on men and journals alike been frankly recognised from the beginning there would not now be a widely-felt sense of irritation, which no amount of success in minor matters can appease. This morning the *Matin* publishes a full and unexpurgated interview, in which Mr. Hughes, of Australia, repeats his clear-cut opinions as to the manner in which the Council of Ten has treated the claim of his country. Three days ago it was stated in this place that in the name of Australia he refused to accept a mandate of which the nature could not possibly be imposed by men whose names had not even been mentioned. In this morning's interview he deals at greater length and more detail with what he conceives to be the only possible attitude of his continent upon questions connected with the allocation of the German colonies. It is a definite challenge, of which the most interesting aspect is that Mr. Hughes has unquestionably with him the sympathy of France.

"NOTHING DECIDED."

He asserts that the question of the German colonies has not received any satisfactory solution, except in the sense that nothing has been decided at all. The vague relegation of a mandate to the as yet unborn League he dismisses as a thing to which no consent on the part of his people is or will be possible. It is not against the theory of a mandate that Australia sets her face; it is against the complete vagueness and instability of the situation which she is asked to accept. It may not be possible for the League to act for years. Meanwhile the continent cannot wait.

Mr. Hughes then called to witness the magnificent valour and enormous sacrifices of life and treasure which had been willingly borne by the Australians from the first moment of the war. "We, at least, did not come to the help of civilisation at the fifteenth hour of the day." This was a strong, perhaps an unnecessarily strong, word. But for saying it Mr. Hughes will not be criticised by Frenchmen. He has cleared the air, and there lies a greater hope of harmony in future than had this warning not been given to the ten idealists. However entrancing the vision of a long-waited-for millennium, the men and women of France, and, I may add, the men of the British Army, too, will allow free speech to the spokesman of those who saved the day, and saved the campaign on that awful day to the east of Amiens not yet a year ago. Was that an occasion when there was time to wait for a mandate from some tribunal in the clouds? "Those men are dead. It seems now that the procedure for which they gave their lives was all wrong."

There is also reported to-day in the Parisian papers the existence of serious disagreement as to the abandonment of the Monroe Doctrine by President Wilson. It seems that the Republicans are quite unwilling to accept the burden of perpetual intervention in the affairs of the Old World. They are equally unwilling that the Old World should interfere with those of the New. Yet without the abolition of the Monroe Doctrine, the League of Nations is merely a beautiful hope. It would be to the benefit of all concerned if the wishes and determination of the Republican majority of the United States were daily and fully published in Paris. We should then know what is probably the most important factor in this equation of many quantities. The censorship of American cable to Paris must be abolished.

A full report of Mr. Hughes's remarks appears on Page Seven.

MANDATE OR POSSESSION

MR. HUGHES'S DECLARATION

PARIS, Sunday.

The *Matin* publishes an account of an interview which M. Lauzanne has had with Mr. Hughes, who is reported to have said:

The Press states that a satisfactory settlement has been reached in the matter of the destinies of the German colonies. A satisfactory settlement. There has been no settlement at all, and if there is any satisfaction, it is at having come to no conclusion. I appeal to the commonsense of everyone. You come to take up the lease of a house or a flat that you require. You ask if the house is unlet, what the rent is, and what other charges there may be. You get the answer: "We can't tell you anything. A board which is going to meet in one or three years will fix the rent and the terms of the lease." Is that a settlement? I ask: Is it a settlement? Well, that is what the Conference has decided upon adding, it is true, that it is provisional. Provisional or not, I know, in any case, that I have not assented to it, and that I shall not do so. Mind; we in Australia have no objections to the theory of a mandate; that Colonial territory is only to be allotted in virtue of the mandate of a delegation of all the civilised nations. That may be so; but then, let them define that mandate, and let them give it now. For us the league of civilised nations is that which is now meeting at the Quai d'Orsay, the one which saved civilisation, when it was at the point of death. It is not a league about which nobody knows when it will be working, and who will belong to it. According to all the precepts of earthly law, the court of justice before which you are pleading ought not to refuse to give judgment, and to refer you to another court, which does not exist, and does not sit, but may some day exist and sit.

M. Lauzanne asked: You refuse to wait?

Mr. Hughes replied: I refuse to wait when they won't even tell me who the judges are that will decide my case, and, again, the question of New Guinea is for us one of life and death. There is no need for me to tell France, at any rate, that for certain peoples, situated in certain geographical conditions, frontier problems have exceptional gravity. It is no question of conquest or Imperialism or aggrandisement for them. It is a matter of knowing whether their territory is to be safe or sound, or is to be given over to all the fancies of passers-by, to all the aggressions of marauders.

Referring to the sacrifices made by Australia, Mr. Hughes is represented to have said: "It is sometimes said that that those who were far off did not understand at once in 1914 the grandeur of the cause for which the world was tearing itself to pieces. We were far off, and we understood at once. It was not half-way through the struggle that we hastened to the defence of civilisation. We had a population of 5,000,000 men, and we armed a tenth of them. From the beginning until the end of the tragedy we had six fighting divisions on the front, without counting one in Asia Minor. We suffered heavier losses than the whole of America; 255,000 of our sons were either killed, crippled, or wounded. Never was an appeal to their courage and devotion made in vain. In the dark days of March, 1918, it was an Australian division that assisted to fill the breach, re-weld the line, and save Amiens. When this division was called upon to make sacrifices it did not reply: "Wait until an international tribunal meets to institute a system of control and give us a mandate." No; our sons responded immediately, without hesitation, without quibbling, and without arguing—responded with their flesh and blood. But now they are dead it seems that the procedure in virtue of which they gave their lives was a bad one. To indemnify them a new one is to be established—remote and slow. Not now is the destiny of the world going to be decided. That will come later. It is to be the task of arbiters, I know not who they are to be, when they are to come, or whence.—*Reuter*.

Australian farmers at the
Royal Agricultural Show, Cardiff

A call came to me from London Headquarters and I was told that I had been detailed to take part in an interesting project. The War Office, as a gesture, had invited and arranged to provide for five hundred Canadian farmers, the same number of Australians, and one hundred each of New Zealand and South African farmers to attend the first Royal Agricultural Show for nearly five years. It was being held at Cardiff in Wales. The War Office was providing a camp and catering facilities free and I was to take charge of the Australian contingent. What an exciting job to be given! I was to proceed at once to Cardiff and see a representative of the War Office there, to consult with the Lord Mayor of Cardiff, and combine with other representatives of the dominion parties in arranging for the reception of the contingents.

The Royal Show had a distinct social side to it. The landed gentry who had exhibits were there in force (it was the thing to do). They came with their servants, cooks and even the butler, and entertained in marquees erected in grounds near to the show area. Lunch was a continuous function and so were the drinks as the succession of visitors from other participating exhibitors paid courtesy calls on each other. I was given the entree by quite a number of these 'exhibitors' and fully availed myself of this courtesy.

To bring the troops back and forth the War Office arranged for special trains to run out to our camp about seven miles from Cardiff where the contingents were billeted.

I was provided with a car and W.A.A.C. driver who was in daily attendance on me, calling for me at the camp in the morning and driving me back in the evening and also to various functions during the day.

The War Office representatives could not have been more attentive to all our needs. It was evident that they had been briefed well, for at the conclusion of the Show the senior War Office representative invited me to accompany him in an official call on the Lord Mayor of Cardiff. He did not inform me what this was for and I thought it would only be a courtesy call but when I got there, to my embarrassment, he 'told off' the Lord Mayor for not showing a greater personal interest in 'our overseas kinsmen'. 'He had not put on anything special for them nor had he even visited them.' This had been reported to the War Office and he had come down from London especially to see the Lord Mayor and get him to do something about it.

The poor man—I felt sorry for him. He had plenty to do with all the other functions he had to attend to without worrying about 'the colonials'. There were many receptions including a most lavish Lord Mayoral dinner to which I, as O.C. Australian Contingent, had the privilege of being invited. The Prince of Wales was the Guest of Honour. This alone was enough for any Lord Mayor to attend to.

The Lord Mayor was very upset and apologetic.

It was too late to do anything with the Canadians or the others as they were returning to their bases very early the next morning, he said. And what about the Australians? Well, I said, I could hold up our return until later in the day. I could have them all assembled at 10 a.m. if he would care to visit us.

This was arranged and next morning he arrived in full regalia preceded by his Mace Bearer, Town Clerk and several attendants. I called the parade to attention, then to stand at ease as he came among us, shaking hands here and there. And then he said he would like to address us. We gathered around in a more or less hollow square and listened to a most eulogistic address in which he praised the work of Australian troops, their marvellous bravery and all that they had done to help the Mother Country in her crisis, finishing with a loudly voiced expression of gratitude to the Almighty for 'sending us the Australians'. 'I thank God for that,' he repeated. The Mace Bearer, standing in front of the Lord Mayor with the mace leaning over his shoulder, kept nodding and tilting the mace forward and downwards to emphasize every laudatory statement the Lord Mayor made. Then turning towards the civilian crowd that had gathered in the background, the Lord Mayor called out, 'Three cheers for the Australians', and these were given enthusiastically. A Digger, feeling the emotion of the moment but, I think, a bit facetiously too, shouted, 'And three cheers for the old Lord Mayor himself!'—which were heartily given by the Diggers.

After the departure of the troops next day I called on the Lord Mayor to make my own farewell and thank him for his courtesy visit to us. He then asked me: 'Did they like my address, was it appreciated and did I cover everything?'

'Very much,' I said. 'Did your hear the Digger call out three cheers for the old Lord Mayor himself?'

'I did so, and that is a compliment that I will always remember and be grateful for receiving!'

That ended the last of the formal British farewell gestures and the shouted words 'three cheers for the Australians' were a tribute that carried a wealth of emotional feeling from our kinsmen of the Mother Country.

Bibliography

BEAN, C. E. W. *Official History of Australia in the War 1914–18*, vols. v, vi: *The A.I.F. in France 1918*. Angus and Robertson, Sydney, 1937, 1942.

BEAN, C. E. W. *Anzac to Amiens: A Shorter History of the Australian Fighting Forces in the First World War.* Australian War Memorial, Sydney, 1946.

BLAXLAND, GREGORY. *Amiens: 1918*. Frederick Muller, London, 1968.

CUTLACK, F. M. *War Letters of General Monash*. Angus & Robertson, Sydney, 1934.

MONASH, (LT.-GENERAL SIR) JOHN. *The Australian Victories in France in 1918*. Hutchinson, London, 1920.

PITT, BARRIE. *1918 — the Last Act*. Cassells, London, 1962.

WIGMORE, L. G. (ed., in collaboration with B. Harding). *They Dared Mightily*. Australian War Memorial, Canberra, 1963.